1978

CONFRONTING YOUTH CRIME

CONFRONTING YOUTH CRIME

Report of the
Twentieth Century Fund
Task Force on
Sentencing Policy Toward
Young Offenders

Background Paper by
Franklin E. Zimring

HM

HOLMES & MEIER PUBLISHERS, INC.
New York   London

Library of Congress Cataloging in Publication Data

Twentieth Century Fund. Task Force on Sentencing Policy
    Toward Young Offenders.
    Confronting Youth Crime.

    1. Juvenile justice, Administration of—United States. 2. Sentences (Criminal procedure)—United States. 3. Prison sentences—United States. I. Zimring, Franklin E. II. Title.
HV9104.T87   1978   364.6   78-3612
ISBN 0-8419-0381-6
ISBN 0-8419-0382-4 pbk.

Contents

Foreword

A decade ago, law and order became a highly politicized issue, in part because crime was demonstrably on the rise and in part because political extremists were concentrating their attacks on law enforcement agencies and the criminal justice system. Ten years of public controversy on this issue have produced a vast quantity of rhetoric but also a substantial number of valid and serious questions relating to public policy. It is now generally understood that preventing crime is a complex task that cannot be carried out by the criminal justice system alone. Even if the criminal justice system alone cannot reduce crime rates, it can and must be made more efficient and humane in its treatment of individuals accused or convicted of crimes.

Criminal sentencing is a case in point. Literature about the courts and correctional institutions—some of it written by ex-offenders—alludes to the demoralizing effects of gross disparities in sentences for essentially similar crimes on offenders and the damage done by such apparent injustices to the credibility of the criminal justice system as a whole. To deal with this issue, the Trustees of the Twentieth Century Fund convened an independent Task Force on Criminal Sentencing; the Report of this Task Force, *Fair and Certain Punishment,* which was published two years ago, dealt with the sentencing of adult criminals.

In the course of preparing its Report, the Task Force considered covering juvenile sentencing, in view of the fact that young people are disproportionately represented in the crime statistics. But recognizing the importance and special problems of juvenile sentencing, the group concentrated on sentencing policy in the criminal courts and proposed to the Fund the establishment of a separate Task Force on the sentencing of young offenders. The pages that follow represent the results of action on this proposition. Crime is a young men's and, recently, young women's game, and the crime rate for offenders under twenty-one has risen, over the past two decades, to an alarming level. Sensational publicity has attended a few cases in which youths who committed particularly heinous crimes received trivial sentences or probation and returned to the streets to commit other offenses. There have been charges that the juvenile courts coddle young-sters who are particularly undeserving of gentle treatment and assertions that some adolescent offenders are hardened criminals beyond hope of redemption. At the same time, the public has been made aware of sordid conditions in juvenile correctional institutions, of punitive detention prac-tices, of arbitrary decisions within the framework of indeterminate sen-tencing policies, and of abuses of privacy involving juvenile court records. These issues were deliberated over by a distinguished group of specialists and concerned citizens—many with extensive experience in the field of criminal justice—who were brought together last spring to form the Fund's independent Task Force on Sentencing Policy Toward Young Offenders.

Despite substantial divergence in affiliations and approaches, the Task Force achieved agreement on the basic outlines of a sentencing policy that is both coherent and innovative. Perhaps its outstanding feature is its transcendence of the preoccupation of past reform efforts with the juvenile court alone. The Task Force recognizes that, if sentencing policy is to become rational and to be perceived as just, the treatment that young offenders receive in adult courts must not be inconsistent with that meted out in the juvenile courts. The Task Force has sought both to bridge this gap and to ensure that young offenders are held responsible—to the extent that level of maturity permits—for their actions.

The Fund is grateful to the entire Task Force for its work and coopera-tion. Robert Taft, Jr., as chairman of the group, played a particularly important role in achieving agreement on a number of issues. Franklin E. Zimring, as rapporteur and author of the background paper, provided an intellectual framework for the Task Force's deliberations, organizing the profusion of ideas that the Task Force members generated into a set of principles to which most could give their assent.

The recommendations of the Task Force will not put an end to the controversy surrounding juvenile justice. But I am confident that they will bring clarity and fresh insights to an area where both are sorely needed.

M. J. Rossant, DIRECTOR
The Twentieth Century Fund
January 1978

Members of the Task Force

Robert A. Taft, Jr.,
chairman,
former Senator from Ohio;
attorney, Taft, Stettinius
  and Hollister,
Washington, D. C.

Allan Breed,
visiting fellow,
Law Enforcement
  Assistance Administration,
Washington, D.C.

Elizabeth Douvan,
social psychologist,
Institute of Social Research,
University of Michigan

Peter B. Edelman,
New York State
  Commissioner of
  Youth Administration

Sister M. Isolina Ferre, M.S.B.T.,
executive director,
Center for
  Orientation and Services,
Puerto Rico

Richard H. Kuh,
attorney, Warshaw, Sylvester,
  Burstein & Frank,
New York, New York

Paul Lerman,
chairman,
Graduate School of Social Work,
Rutgers University

George Napper,
Crime Analysis Team,
Atlanta, Georgia

Aryeh Neier,
executive director,
American Civil Liberties Union,
New York, New York

Justine Wise Polier,
retired judge,
New York State Family Court

Cruz Reynoso,
justice,
California Appellate Court

William Sylvester White,
judge,
Cook County Circuit Court
  — Juvenile Division

Marvin E. Wolfgang,
director, Center for
  Studies in Criminology,
University of Pennsylvania

Robert L. Woodson,
resident fellow,
American Enterprise Institute,
Washington, D. C.

Franklin E. Zimring,
rapporteur,
professor of law;
director, Center for Studies
  in Criminal Justice,
University of Chicago

Report of
the Task Force

Introduction

Crime in the United States is predominantly the province of the young. Males between the ages of thirteen and twenty—the turbulent years of adolescence—comprise about 9 percent of the population but account for more than half of all property crime arrests and more than a third of all arrests for offenses involving violence. In all Western nations, crime is concentrated among adolescents. But in the United States, where crime rates are high and violent crime is much more widespread than in other developed societies, youth crime is a special problem.

These statistics raise two basic and difficult questions:

- Why is crime so intensely concentrated in the adolescent years?
- Why is violent youth crime so much more prevalent in the United States than in other industrial democracies?

We know some, but not all, of the answers to these questions. The American adolescent, struggling with the biological and psychological pressures of growth, seeks status and reassurance in the company of his peers. Rebellion against parental authority and restrictions is combined with pressure to conform to the expectations of other adolescents. The teen years are a period of experiment, risk-taking, and bravado. Some criminal activity is part of the pattern of almost all youth subcultures. In urban areas, physical mobility and conspicuous materialism increase the volume of crime. Uneven distribution of income, racial segregation, and a culture that makes the tools of violence available contribute to the number of violent offenses by the young and the deaths and injuries that such crimes produce.

Separating Fact from Fiction

Youth crime has always been the subject of public concern; in recent years, it has become a matter of public alarm. Unfortunately, the media

3

and the public tend to focus on sensational cases. Misinformation and emotional rhetoric often substitute for fact in the public debate over crime.

Some basic facts:

- Most young persons violate the law at some point during adolescence; relatively few young persons are repetitive, serious criminals.
- Most youth crime is not violent crime; offenses involving property outnumber violent crimes by more than ten to one; yet violent crime by the young has increased and is a substantial social and public health problem.
- Most violent crime by the young is committed against young victims; a substantial amount of violence also spills over to other age groups, and about 10 percent of all robbery by young offenders involves elderly victims.
- Most young persons who commit serious offenses will outgrow the propensity to commit crime in the transition to adulthood; a significant minority of serious young offenders will persist in criminal careers.
- Most young offenders who commit acts of extreme violence and pursue criminal careers come from minority ghettos and poverty backgrounds; so do their victims.
- Youth crime has increased dramatically over the past fifteen years, in part because of the growth of the youth population in large urban areas that have been incubators of crime; in the next few years, youth crime rates will probably not continue to grow at the pace of recent years because the total youth population will decline and the minority youth population in most major cities will remain relatively stable.*

This Task Force is concerned with sentencing policy toward the large number and great variety of young offenders arrested each year. Our mission is broader than the reform of juvenile justice in the sense that it encompasses all adolescents accused of crimes—both those youths who are sent to criminal court and those who are sent to juvenile court.

Too often, efforts to reform juvenile justice have ignored the treatment of young offenders in criminal courts. The boundary between the juvenile court—whose task, in theory, is to provide help and guidance for those who come under its jurisdiction—and criminal court—where the young

*The sources on which these conclusions are based, and the difficulties inherent in the confident use of existing sources of data are discussed in Chapter I of the background paper,

offender is usually subject to the full range of criminal sanctions but also is entitled to a jury trial and the full range of appeals—is both arbitrary and subject to abrupt change. The maximum age of juvenile court jurisdiction varies in the United States from under sixteen to under nineteen. In the past five years, no fewer than ten of the fifty states have changed the maximum—some raising it and others lowering it. **The Task Force is convinced that no single age during mid-adolescence should be used as a sharp dividing line for sentencing policies. We have considered sentencing policy toward young offenders in both juvenile and criminal courts and recommend coordinating the policies of these two institutions so that public policy toward young offenders is based on consistent and coherent premises.**

The mission of this Task Force is also narrower than that of some other recent law reform study commissions, which have dealt with the entire range of behavior that is currently under the jurisdiction of the juvenile court.[1] This Report focuses on youth crimes with discernible victims—crimes against property and personal safety—and on the sanctioning decision rather than on the reform of procedures for fact-finding and court organization.

The rate of youth crime is largely determined by factors outside the justice system—social forces that fix the meaning of adolescence, economic opportunity, racial mobility, and cultural values in the milieu of the adolescent and in the larger social order, which he or she has done little to shape. The Task Force believes that sentencing policy is, at most, one of many conditions that determine the quantity and severity of youth crime in the United States.

Moreover, **no sentencing policy is any better than the facilities we use to deal with the young offender.** The facilities provided for the young— within and without the community—must be adequate and humane. No matter how carefully crafted, no sentencing system makes sense if the adolescent offender is sent to a mega-prison such as Stateville or Attica.

The Task Force has struggled to reconcile society's need to shelter the young with its equally strong need to deal with serious crime. We do not view the details of our proposals as a definitive solution confidently derived from first principles but as a step toward rationality and consistency in an area where there are no totally right answers.

Rethinking Basic Premises

The establishment of the juvenile court in 1899 was a dramatic innovation in social policy toward youth crime. The purpose of the juvenile court was not to dispense justice to criminals but to identify and meet the needs of "delinquents." Because the juvenile court would exercise state power only benignly, the judge was given discretion to sentence any delinquent to anything from probation through institutional confinement—until his or her majority. And because the label of delinquency was to carry no stigma, almost any troubled youth could be found delinquent.

In practice, however, the label of "juvenile delinquent" does carry a stigma. And the power to confine and supervise can be abused. The arbitrary boundary between the juvenile and the criminal court places too much importance on a single birthday, and legislatures have differed as to when criminal responsibility should begin. A child in New Jersey is an adult in New York, and very few states make special provision for the treatment of young offenders in criminal courts.

The theory behind the juvenile court is not merely obsolete; it is a fairy tale that never came true. The court has helped some young offenders, but it has punished others. From the beginning, juvenile court judges have considered the interests of the state as well as those of the offender. It is pointless to pretend that social policy toward youth crime is based solely on the best interests of the young offender or that the best interests of the offender and those of the state are always the same. But the juvenile court need not rely on hypocritical rhetoric to justify its jurisdiction over youths charged with crimes.

Foundations for a Special Youth Crime Policy

In fashioning and justifying a discrete policy toward youth crime, the Task Force has been guided by four principles:

- culpability
- diminished responsibility resulting from immaturity
- providing room to reform
- proportionality.

Culpability.   When six-year-olds steal or set fires, the legal system correctly recognizes that extreme immaturity should operate as a complete defense to criminal responsibility. In its deliberations, the Task Force did not consider the appropriate minimum age at which children should become partially responsible for threatening social behavior. **The Task Force did decide that at age thirteen or fourteen, an individual may appropriately be considered responsible, at least to a degree, for the criminal harms that he or she causes.**

The moral universe of early adolescence is complicated, but a basic sense of right and wrong is a part of that stage of development. **We feel that most young offenders of that age are aware of the severity of the** criminal harms they inflict and that, much as they fall short of maturity or self-control, they are morally and should be legally responsible for intentionally destructive behavior. The older the adolescent, the greater the degree of responsibility the law should presume. Whether criminal behavior on the part of adolescents should be called delinquency or crime is of little consequence to this conclusion and was not a subject on which the Task Force took a position.

Diminished Responsibility.   In reaching the conclusion that young offenders should be legally responsible for intentional criminal harms, the Task Force relied on its opinion that adolescent offenders have moral judgment and varying degrees of capacity for self-control. At the same time, the Task Force recognizes that adolescents, particularly in the early and middle teen years, are more vulnerable, more impulsive, and less self-disciplined than adults. Crimes committed by youths may be just as harmful to victims as those committed by older persons, but they deserve less punishment because adolescents may have less capacity to control their conduct and to think in long-range terms than adults. Moreover, youth crime as such is not exclusively the offender's fault; offenses by the young also represent a failure of family, school, and the social system, which share responsibility for the development of America's youth.

The Task Force believes that a balanced sentencing policy toward young offenders must recognize both culpability and its limits. It is unrealistic to view a sixteen-year-old as completely devoid of judgment and control; it is equally unrealistic to treat young offenders as if they have fully mature judgment and control.

Providing room to reform.   The Task Force believes that protecting young offenders from the full force of the criminal law is prudent social policy. Many forms of youth crime are a product of the special pressures and vulnerability of adolescence. This is why adolescent rates of crime are high and why persons who have violated the law in their youth usually desist from criminality as they grow up. The Task Force assigns a high priority to providing young offenders with the opportunity to pass through this crime-prone stage of development with their life chances intact.

Providing room to reform simply means using procedures that minimize stigma, custodial confinement, and exile from society. In advocating such a policy, the Task Force does not mean to imply that young criminal recidivists should go unpunished. The treatment encountered by young offenders inevitably serves an educational function, and the last thing the Task Force would wish young people to learn is that criminal behavior goes unpunished. In some cases (fewer than many suppose), protecting the young offender from being scarred by severe punishment is inappropriate. But in general, giving young offenders a chance to reform is intelligent social policy. Such a policy involves risks and costs; a considerable minority of young offenders may not outgrow their propensity to crime. But there is no evidence that secure confinement is more effective than lesser measures in dissuading young offenders from pursuing criminal careers.

Proportionality.   No coherent theory of criminal justice that acknowledges punishment as an appropriate response to crime can treat bank robbers and bicycle thieves as equal for the purpose of punishment. "Proportionality" is not a magic slogan that automatically produces consensus on appropriate punishment. **But the Task Force believes that the degree of punishment available for youth crime should be proportional to the seriousness of the offense.*** The point seems obvious, but proportionality is not an integral part of the present jurisprudence of juvenile justice. We believe it should be.

The Dual System of Justice—Abolition or Reform?

At present, an adolescent accused of a crime may be processed in one of two court systems: younger adolescents are tried in juvenile court and older adolescents in criminal court. The Task Force debated the issue of whether a child-centered court is appropriate for processing serious criminal charges against fifteen- to seventeen-year-olds. The alternative to this "dual" system would be the abolition of juvenile court jurisdiction for felony charges and the referral of such charges to either the criminal court or a special court for young offenders. **We concluded that, although the principles and processes of the juvenile court require rethinking and reform, juvenile court jurisdiction over individuals in their mid-teens is preferable to alternatives.****

Shifting jurisdiction to a special "court for young offenders" would

---

*Peter Edelman comments: While I agree that the concept of proportionality should be applied to youth sentencing policy, I want to state explicitly that I am opposed to the full-fledged "miniaturization" of the adult system, as represented by some recent proposals. Differentiation is certainly appropriate as between violent acts and property crime, and perhaps between repeated serious property crime and other property crime, but further distinctions at the sentencing level, given the relatively short time frames that are appropriate for young offenders, seem to me highly artificial.

Justine Wise Polier wishes to associate with this comment.

**Marvin Wolfgang comments: However, for *serious* offenders, at least, the sanctioning process should be the same as that used for adults.

simply apply a new label to an institution quite similar to the contemporary juvenile court.

For the purpose of processing accused youths, juvenile court has two advantages over criminal court: the judge before whom the accused appears is likely to have a special concern for and some experience with young persons and, if detained, the accused is likely to be placed in age-segregated facilities.

Although a juvenile detention facility is typically not a satisfactory place to house a young person accused of an offense, it is far more satisfactory than a jail. And for those convicted, although "training schools" neither train nor school, they are less destructive than the crowded and dangerous mega-prisons used to warehouse older offenders. A separate court should not be needed to assure diverse correctional treatment. **Indeed, the Task Force recommends that even those young offenders who are convicted in criminal courts should be placed in age-segregated facilities.** But separate, specialized, and decent facilities are more easily achieved with the juvenile court than without it.

Jurisdictional Age and Waiver

If the juvenile court is to continue, some boundary line must be established between those who will be processed by the juvenile court and those who will be processed by the criminal court. For most arrested young persons, this line is the maximum age of juvenile court jurisdiction; a few persons still young enough to go to the juvenile court but accused of serious offenses may stand trial in the criminal court, depending on the waiver policies of the state in which they are tried.

The Task Force recommends that juvenile court jurisdiction extend to all criminal acts committed before an accused's eighteenth birthday.* Eighteen is not the end of adolescence (it may be a rough boundary between middle and late adolescence), and it should not mark the end of a special sentencing policy toward youth crime. Hence, although eighteen- to twenty-one-year-old defendants should be tried in criminal courts and eligible for higher maximum sanctions than those in juvenile court, the sanctions available for individuals in this age group should be lower than those for adults. Thus, the passage from juvenile to adult court would be a transition from one youth crime policy to another—somewhat less lenient—youth crime policy.

Any large jurisdiction that retains young offenders until age eighteen will encounter a few extremely serious offenses that will seem, to the court and

---

*Marvin Wolfgang dissents: If the juvenile court is kept, jurisdiction should not extend beyond, at most, age sixteen.

the community, to demand more substantial punishment than is normally available to the juvenile justice system. State law can provide for these "deep-end" cases in three ways: by lowering the maximum age of juvenile court jurisdiction (typically to under sixteen or seventeen), by increasing the sentencing authority of the juvenile court, or by providing for the transfer of cases to the criminal court.

The minimum age for criminal court jurisdiction might be lowered either for all crimes or for specific offenses such as murder and rape. Generally lowering the jurisdictional age would burden the adult system with thousands of cases in order to cope with the problems posed by a few. Offense-specific reduction of jurisdictional age would be less objectionable, but it would require categorical judgments regarding accessories as well as principal offenders. Moreover, the publicizing of atypical, sensational cases may result in amendments to a legislative list of heinous crimes, lengthening it to include crimes that are generally less serious.

Expanding the punishment power of the juvenile court also has disadvantages. First, it bases the punitive outer limits of the court on a few exceptional cases, virtually letting the tail wag the dog in setting sentencing policy. Second, it puts too great a burden on the procedural structure of the juvenile court. A court that does not provide access to jury trial should not be able to impose five- or ten-year sentences. Juvenile court is unlikely to establish a full array of procedural formalities for all cases; attempts to make it do so would be another instance of letting the few exceptional cases set policy for the bulk of the court's work.

The Task Force believes that the least harmful method of dealing with extremely serious cases is to transfer them to the criminal court. The process we recommend differs from the present practice of waiver in two respects. First, under current practice in most states, the judge makes the decision to waive at his discretion, without any explicit standard for guidance. **We would confine waiver to cases where the judge finds probable cause to believe that a serious, violent crime has been committed and further determines that, should the defendant be found guilty, the minimum punishment necessary is substantially larger than that available to the juvenile court.** The waiver decision would be automatically reviewed by an appellate tribunal (unless the defendant and his counsel elected to give up this right), which could nullify the decision to transfer to criminal court if the basis for the juvenile court's finding were not clear and convincing.

A second distinction between present practice and our proposal concerns the consequences of transfer to the criminal court. At present, waiver to criminal court means eligibility for the full range of maximum adult sentences, including life in prison or the death penalty. **Under our proposal, the juvenile transferred to criminal court would have the same** status that we propose for young offenders eighteen to twenty-one. Juveniles in the criminal court would thus face increased maximum sanctions, but the legal system would not totally ignore their youth in setting punishment.

The Task Force also recommends that waiver be restricted to defendants who are accused of serious criminal violence and who have passed their early teens. We are unanimous in recommending that very young adolescents should not be eligible for transfer to criminal court. A majority of the Task Force favors a bar on the transfer to criminal court of any child under age fifteen.*

The Sentencing Structure

The Task Force considered a variety of models of sentencing structure. **We recommend a system of sentencing in which** *the legislature* **fixes the maximum period of loss of liberty and supervision,** *the judge* **retains discretion to determine whether or not the offender should be subjected to loss of liberty and to fix the maximum duration of social control in each individual case, and** *a centralized correctional authority* **retains the power to select a release date short of the maximum.**** Some members of the Task Force who endorse this system believe that an early

---

*Sister M. Isolina Ferre, M.S.B.T., dissents: I oppose waiver of juveniles to the adult criminal justice system under any conditions because, given the chaotic state of the criminal courts, neither the public nor the individual youth can benefit more from criminal court processing than from juvenile court processing.

Moreover, any use of waiver subjects juveniles to a system of justice based on "category of offense" rather than on concern with the individual and with the social and cultural aspects of the case. Such concern is the principal virtue of the juvenile justice system.

**Peter Edelman comments: While I endorse this distribution of responsibility, I also would stress that what the correctional authority should retain is the power to select a facility or program for the offender as well as a release date short of the maximum. In cases of serious violent acts, I believe that judges should have the power to require a minimum period of secure confinement; otherwise, I think the nature of the loss of liberty should be up to the correctional authority. Especially where youth are concerned, "custody," "loss of liberty," and "social control" should not be equated with institutionalization or incarceration. I take these terms to encompass placement in group homes or other community-based residences, in family foster care, or even in a youth's own home with adequate professional supervision.

Aryeh Neier dissents: I believe that the length of a sentence should depend on the underlying crime. The trial judge is best informed about that crime and, accordingly, should fix the length of the sentence. Correctional authorities, such as parole boards, currently base decisions regarding early release on predictions about the individual inmate's future behavior. Such predictions are unreliable and unfair. Elsewhere, the report rejects rehabilitation as a purpose of confinement (although it favors providing opportunities for rehabilitation to people in confinement). Allowing a correctional authority to alter release dates on the basis of a subjective judgment as to the psychological state of the inmate implies that rehabilitation is a valid objective of confinement.

release decision of the correctional authority should be subject to the approval of the sentencing judge.

In our deliberations, we considered and rejected presumptive, or legislatively fixed, sentences as inappropriate to most young offenders in both juvenile and criminal courts.* The Task Force also considered and rejected indeterminate sentences, in which a young offender's confinement ends only when a correctional authority feels that the offender has been reformed. Although rehabilitation and helping services are a necessary part of any rational scheme of dealing with young offenders, **the Task Force believes that the need for services should not be used to justify placing a young offender in custodial confinement or continuing such confinement until an administrative agency considers him "cured."**

In recommending an allocation of sentencing authority that retains a substantial amount of discretion for judges and correctional authorities, the Task Force recognizes that this discretion carries with it the danger of disparity in sentences. Some of the policy recommendations and the maximum sentences suggested later in the report are designed to reduce the risk of disparity. The sharing of power between the sentencing judge and a central correctional authority can lead toward less variation in sentences for similar offenders. Unfortunately, the flexibility that is the virtue of a discretionary policy can still result in abuses. But in the sentencing policy we propose, we have sought to minimize the use of secure confinement, to retain discretion, and to provide mechanisms for reducing disparity.**

Sentences for Young Property Offenders

At present, there are no legislative or administrative guidelines to govern the hundreds of thousands of property offenders who are referred to the juvenile court and few principles to guide criminal courts in dealing with the

I do not mean to preclude prison officials from modifying sentences slightly in recognition of good behavior. The availability of this incentive may aid correctional authorities in exercising their managerial responsibilities. The distinction I am drawing is between the subjective judgment that a person is rehabilitated and will not commit crimes if released and a more objective evaluation of past behavior as, in itself, justifying early release.

*Marvin Wolfgang dissents: I am not prepared to reject presumptive sentences as strong guides for all offenders.

**Marvin Wolfgang comments: I am troubled by the degree to which the sentencing structure proposed by the Task Force retains discretion. Such discretion invites sentencing disparity in both juvenile and criminal courts. Recently, mechanisms, such as sentencing guidelines and—for some cases—presumptive sanctions, have been proposed for the criminal court. As I read this Task Force Report, it does not foreclose the use of these promising reform mechanisms. But I would go further and suggest that presumptive sanctions or greatly narrowed sentencing discretion should be a major objective of sentencing reform in both juvenile and criminal justice.

adolescent property offender. In its deliberations, the Task Force reached a substantial consensus on appropriate policy toward these high-volume, youth-dominated crimes.

Property Offenders in Juvenile Court. **The Task Force concluded (with one dissent) that the juvenile court should retain jurisdiction over all defendants accused of nonviolent offenses.** For all property offenses except burglary of a dwelling, the Task Force favors an administrative presumption that juveniles who have not previously been arrested for a serious offense should be handled informally. The shock of arrest, a stern admonition by judge or intake worker, and referral to helping services are regarded as an adequate response to the first-arrested vandal, shoplifter, thief, or joyrider, although formal handling of a case may be thought necessary in some instances.

The Task Force considers burglarizing a dwelling too serious an incident to justify a presumption of informal handling. Other forms of burglary and vandalism that involve substantial fear or property loss may also merit formal handling.

If an offender is arrested a second time for a serious property crime, the Task Force recommends that the presumption should shift; most cases should proceed to a formal hearing on the defendant's guilt and to a subsequent dispositional hearing. If the defendant is found guilty, the Task Force favors a presumption against custodial confinement for young persons first convicted on property charges. The Task Force also supports a one-year limit on custodial confinement and a two-year limit on total state-imposed power as the maximum sanction for property offenders in juvenile court.

The Task Force considers repetitive property crime by juveniles a serious matter. Limiting the use of secure confinement generates a need to find other less drastic means of censuring such offenders. A wide variety of such alternatives is available in many juvenile justice systems, and **the Task Force recommends the expanded use of sanctions that impress on the offender the seriousness of his conduct but do less harm than detention homes and training schools.** Among promising intermediate sanctions, the Task Force identified the following:

- restitution programs, in which the young offender's efforts or resources are used to offset at least a part of the losses he caused

- community service orders, in which young offenders work for public agencies to atone for offenses that violate social norms

- fines that are geared to an offender's ability to pay, so that the offender rather than his family will bear the financial burden*

- loss of privileges, such as driving, which young people value highly

- participation in remedial educational, drug treatment, or alcohol treatment programs in appropriate cases.**

Many of these approaches are intended to help improve a young offender's life chances. All are coercive exercises of state power that are imposed because the juvenile has committed serious offenses. **The Task Force feels that it is appropriate for the offender and the community to recognize that these measures are imposed, in part, as punishment.** Open recognition of the punitive function of assigned participation in such a program seems preferable to a policy in which the rhetoric of rehabilitation is used to explain decisions that inevitably (and properly) spring in part from punitive motives.

These proposals are a radical departure from present theory but are closer to present practices than the public might believe. In one study of a major urban area, it was found that fewer than one out of fifty auto theft arrests resulted in secure confinement after trial; the odds for an accused burglar were one in twenty-five. A much larger proportion of accused property offenders were detained prior to the adjudication of their charges.[2] Pretrial detention appears to be widely used as punishment for young property offenders in both juvenile and criminal courts. **The Task Force urges the abolition of punitive pretrial detention for juvenile property offenders.**

Young Property Offenders in Criminal Court.   The Task Force believes that it is necessary to coordinate treatment of property offenders in late adolescence with the policies proposed for juveniles. **Specifically, we recommend a presumption against incarceration for first offenders in criminal court, the extensive use of alternative sanctions, and a two-and-a-half-year maximum sentence in custodial confinement** for any property offense committed before the defendant's twenty-first birthday. This scale of punishment includes sentences longer than those available to

---

*Cruz Reynoso dissents: I object to the inclusion of fines as an "intermediate sanction." While the theory that fines should be levied only in terms of the offender's ability to pay is a good one, experience suggests that fines can seldom be levied in a manner that does not "punish" the parents.

**Peter Edelman comments: The key word in this context is "sanction." The enumeration in the text is not intended to exclude use of community-based group care and family foster care as available dispositions. The Task Force took the view that they might be coupled with sanctions but would not be themselves imposed for punitive purposes.

the juvenile court because older adolescents are more mature and should be held more accountable for criminal conduct. But the proposed maximum penalties are lower than those available for adults because the reasons for a separate youth policy do not disappear on an offender's eighteenth birthday.

Sentencing Policy Toward the Violent Young Offender

Youth arrests for police-classified "violent" offenses are less than 10 percent of total youth arrests. These offenses range from fistfights to murder, from schoolyard extortion to life-threatening armed robbery. Most violent crimes that lead to youth arrests are less serious than media coverage suggests, but young offenders are all too frequently involved in armed robbery, life-threatening assaults with deadly weapons, rape, and murder, in that order. Serious violent offenses are the hardest cases for social policy that seeks to protect both young offenders and the community.

In considering sentencing policy toward offenses against the person, the Task Force found it necessary to define three classes of violent offenders. First and most numerous are those who have committed assaults that did not involve serious threats to life or robberies in which the defendant did not personally use a deadly weapon or inflict grave bodily harm. Second are offenses that threaten life or person more directly:

- robbery where the defendant personally used a deadly weapon or inflicted grievous bodily harm

- battery, for which an offender is personally responsible, that involved a firearm, dangerous wounding with a knife, or force that required hospitalization

- voluntary manslaughter

- attempted rape

- accessorial responsibility for class 3 offenses

- arson of a dwelling or of an occupied building.

Third are those offenders personally responsible for:

- murder and attempted murder

- forcible rape

- arson with intent to commit bodily harm.

Violent Offenses in Juvenile Court.   The Task Force recommends a presumption favoring formal processing of all but the most trivial of

offenses against the person. Even within the lowest grade of crimes against the person, only fistfights, schoolyard extortions, and episodes of limited self-defense (overreaction to provocation) may merit less than formal processing.

For the first and least serious class of offenses against the person, the Task Force recommends no minimum sanction and a maximum sentence of eighteen months of custodial confinement or a longer but limited maximum period of noncustodial social control.

For the second and more serious class of offenses against the person, the Task Force believes that minimum sentences of custodial confinement are worthy of serious consideration and that the maximum sentence should be two years of custodial confinement. The Task Force also favors a presumption of waiver to the criminal court for those once convicted of a class 2 offense who are again arrested and are probably guilty of a second such offense.

For class 3 (the most serious) offenses, the Task Force recommends minimum sentences of some custodial confinement and maximum sentences of two-and-a-half years of custodial confinement. The Task Force favors this relatively low maximum because of the procedural frailty of the juvenile court. We believe that cases calling for more fateful punishment decisions should be waived to criminal court, where procedural guarantees that juvenile court does not provide are available.

Youth Violence in Criminal Court.   Crimes against the person test the limits of a separate social policy toward youth crime in the criminal court. The Task Force is unanimous in suggesting that the maximum sentencing options be significantly lower for violent young offenders than those for adults convicted of comparable crimes. We also agree that the case for minimum punishment is stronger for young offenders (and transferred juveniles) in criminal court than for those in the juvenile court.

The Task Force is divided on the question of whether offenders under twenty-one should ever be subject to sentences of over five years for any crime short of murder. This division is not a sign of disarray. Our deliberations on this topic reflected both the difficulty of moving from general principles to specific guidelines and the arbitrary nature of any specific numerical guideline. The debate specifically concerned defendants convicted of repeated instances of class 2 or class 3 violence. Those members of the Task Force who oppose the five-year limit are themselves divided; some favor prescribing some increase in the maximum sentence (e.g., 7½ years); others advocate providing for discretionary waiver to the full range of adult sanctions for repetitive offenders between eighteen and twenty-one. Thus, this division of the Task Force is limited to the issue of whether repetitive, violent young offenders should be subject to a five-year maximum, exempted from a youth crime policy, or subject to longer sentences as part of a youth crime policy.

Murder remains the hardest of the hard cases. The young offender who dominates or commits an intentional killing is the ultimate test of the limits of diminished responsibility. **The Task Force agreed that maximum sanctions for young offenders should be lower than those for adults.** The principle of diminished responsibility makes life imprisonment and death penalties inappropriate in such cases. **The Task Force recommends substantial presumptive minimum sanctions as appropriate because of the gravity of the offense; eighteen months of custodial confinement for offenders under eighteen and three years of custodial confinement for offenders between eighteen and twenty-one.** The Task Force recommends that sentences of over five years for offenders under eighteen convicted of murder and sentences exceeding ten years for offenders between eighteen and twenty-one be confined to cases where the offender is responsible for taking more than one life or has a substantial history of life-threatening violent offenses.

Punitive Detention

Ten times as many juveniles are in secure confinement before trial as after trial, and the purpose of this confinement is, in many cases, punitive. Of course, in criminal courts, too, far more defendants are in jail before trial than after adjudication of charges. **The Task Force considers punitive pretrial detention inappropriate and unjust.**

Any unjust but prevalent practice may be difficult to abolish. The Task Force favors a variety of devices as alternatives to the present high rate of secure detention before trial. **Specifically, we favor community supervision rather than detention to assure that young defendants appear at trial, nonsecure pretrial housing where necessary, and judicial and administrative monitoring of information on detention.** These practices are needed in both branches of the dual system of criminal justice but are particularly necessary in the juvenile court.

Information-Sharing Between Juvenile and Criminal Courts

In many states, outgrowing the juvenile court's jurisdiction may have two paradoxical consequences: instant responsibility and retroactive virginity. As soon as an offender is no longer young enough to be "delinquent," he is treated as an adult fully responsible for his acts. But a number of laws and practices shield records of juvenile adjudication from prosecutors and judges in the adult system. As a result, an individual who has acquired an extensive and serious record in the juvenile court enters the adult system as if he were a first offender. Under these conditions, processing by the adult system may lead to more leniency, for the young offender may receive more lenient treatment in criminal court than he would in juvenile court.

The need for coordination of information between juvenile and adult court systems is clear. And yet, shielding juvenile court records from the public eye serves the valid purpose of protecting the young from permanent stigma. Whatever the proper balance between privacy and information-sharing, the present system probably gives us the worst of both worlds. Juvenile arrest records, perhaps the least reliable indicia of guilt, are not well protected from outside scrutiny. But in most jurisdictions, at the critical early stages of adult prosecution, records of adjudication in the juvenile court are often not available.

The Task Force favors both increased safeguards against the leakage of arrest and juvenile court records and provisions to make certain juvenile court records available to counsel and judges in the criminal court.* Under our proposal, an offender's juvenile court records should be sealed when he reaches eighteen or, if he is confined or under supervision at that time, when the court's jurisdiction over him ends. If, as a juvenile, an individual has been found guilty of a class 2 or class 3 violent offense or has been twice convicted of any felony charge, and is charged with a felony within three years after release from juvenile confinement or three years after passing the jurisdictional age of the court, the record of adjudication should be available to the criminal court. If he is not convicted, his records should be returned to the juvenile court. If he is convicted, his juvenile record should be available thereafter on the same basis as criminal court records.

If, during the first three years after he leaves the jurisdiction of the juvenile court, the young offender is not charged with a felony of which he is found guilty, all his police and juvenile court records should be permanently unavailable thereafter.**

In designing this policy, the Task Force has sought to provide room for the offender to reform without stigma. After three years of arrest-free life in the community, a young offender deserves to be regarded as having outgrown the patterns of adolescent crime portrayed in his juvenile court record. Rapid rearrest is a sign of trouble.

Of course, foolproof schemes to balance privacy with coordination of information are difficult to design. If "sealing" juvenile records does not

---

*Robert Taft, Jr., comments: In addition, a defendant should have access to his own juvenile court record upon request.

**Marvin Wolfgang dissents: I am not in favor of making police and juvenile court records "permanently unavailable." There is nothing magical about three years of escaping arrest and conviction. Self-report studies and low clearance by arrest rates for index crimes make the three-year rule inappropriate. If there is to be a rule at all, ten years would be better.

protect information leaks, the destruction of juvenile records may be worthy of serious consideration. **The Task Force opposes providing information to prosecutors before probable cause hearings because, in the age of the photocopier, the return of a record is no guarantee of privacy. The Task Force feels risk of permanent release of juvenile court records is not justified until a judge has found probable cause to believe the defendant guilty of the subsequent charge. The Task Force also opposes withholding court records until after conviction on the adult charge, because on that basis, most criminal court dispositions would take place before the judge or prosecutor could learn of the defendant's serious prior record. At present, the Task Force hopes that requiring the return of juvenile records will provide sufficient protection of privacy to justify earlier release of juvenile records.**

In making these recommendations, the Task Force assumes that juvenile court jurisdiction extends to age eighteen. Systems with lower age limits should consider more stringent restrictions on the availability of information.

Concluding Reflections

The Task Force, like many other study groups that have preceded its work, is saddened by the low quality of the courts, community facilities, and residential institutions that process and house young offenders in most jurisdictions. In many rural areas, the judge who presides over juvenile court cases is more like a justice of the peace than a specialist in sentencing policy toward young offenders. In many cities, the juvenile court often resembles the local traffic court, and the professional prestige of judges charged with dealing with young offenders is low. These conditions must change.

Most detention, probation, and correctional facilities for young offenders are evidence of social and governmental indifference. The observation that youth correctional facilities are better than their adult counterparts is valid, but small praise. Currently, confinement in age-segregated facilities is necessary but insufficient to assure even decent processing and acceptable housing, let alone appropriate program options.

The need to reform both the principles and the institutions that confront the young offender is particularly acute because juvenile and criminal courts are an important source of the image of justice perceived by young offenders. They learn from their experience in courts and correctional institutions. They are influenced most by what actually happens to them and how it happens; by what is done rather than by what is supposed to be done; by the attitudes and actions of the police, corrections officers, and magistrates, not by ringing declarations about justice or by leather-bound statute books.

In most juvenile and criminal courts, young offenders learn the hypocrisy of punishment in the name of rehabilitation, of disparity in the cloak of individualized justice, and of assembly line treatment in the guise of informality. Young offenders are not easy to trick. Candor and consistency in sentencing policy are a first and fundamental step toward instilling respect for law and legal institutions in young persons whose respect for law is a critical element of their personal futures and the safety of our communities.*

*Sister M. Isolina Ferre, M.S.B.T., dissents: The administration of the criminal and juvenile justice systems is largely in the hands of the white community. Those most affected by these systems are black and Hispanic. The Task Force has failed to consider this issue or to recommend measures to bring black and Hispanic people into the criminal justice system so that they can participate in decisions that affect their own people. This omission leaves the Task Force Report open to criticism as a racist document.

Notes

1.   See, for example, Institute of Judicial Administration/American Bar Association, Juvenile Justice Standards and Goals project (a thirty-six volume effort of which nine volumes have been published). See also American Justice Institute, *A Comparative Analysis of Standards and State Practices* (nine volumes) (Washington, D.C.: U.S. Government Printing Office, 1977) (prepared for National Institute for Juvenile Justice and Delinquency Prevention, Office of Juvenile Justice and Delinquency Prevention, Law Enforcement Assistance Administration, Department of Justice).

2.   Data provided by June Dorn, Illinois Law Enforcement Commission.

DISSENT by Richard H. Kuh

At a time when the overall trend in the criminal justice system is toward firmer punishment policies, the Task Force calls for (or perpetuates), at least in large part, a pattern of leniency toward youth crime. And in its consideration of "youth crime," the Task Force construes the word "youth" very broadly. Were the term applied solely to those whom I have heretofore regarded as juveniles—youngsters who have not reached puberty or those who have attained it within three or four years—I would have no problem with such a lenient approach. But the Task Force has applied the term to individuals as old as twenty. Quite apart from the facts that eighteen-year-olds today can vote and that those between eighteen and twenty-one, most typically, are working or able to work or completing college, are sexually and physically mature (and, mentally, close to being as mature as they will ever be), and are in many cases married or the equivalent—the Task Force itself recognizes that this age group is responsible for much of the crime that continues to scourge our society. Thus, the opening sentence of the Report states:

> Crime in the United States is predominantly the province of the young. Males between the ages of thirteen and twenty—the turbulent years of adolescence—comprise about 9 percent of the population but account for more than half of all property crime arrests and more than a third of all arrests for offenses involving violence.

The Report also states: "the last thing the Task Force would wish young people to learn is that criminal behavior goes unpunished."

Having, in this fashion, correctly noted both the importance of not teaching the young their criminal behavior will go unpunished and that one-third to one-half of crime in the United States appears to be attributable to the acts of the young, the Task Force moves on to recommendations that, in my view, fly in the face of these valid observations. Thus, in essence, the Task

21

Force recommends that individuals under age eighteen, committing property crimes that would be felonies under the appropriate statutes were the offenders older (which crimes, for simplicity, I will hereinafter term felonies), not ordinarily even be brought into court for the first such felony, not be sentenced to detention for the second, and receive, at most, sharply circumscribed punishment for the third! Were the Report to serve as a template for state laws, it would effectively put the young on official notice that the state's policy was not to punish nonviolent criminal behavior—at least for the first two arrests. This policy would not serve to deter nonviolent youth crime.

Penology, increasingly, appears to recognize that sentences of imprisonment are likely to have little deterrent effect on adult offenders and that, for the sake of candor, society should make the retributive function of sentencing explicit. Young offenders are less acceptable as objects of vengeance than older offenders, but they may be more readily deterred from crime by the idea of prison than older offenders. The young are generally viewed as malleable; both parents and teachers use punishment to improve behavior. And so I bridle at the Report's general rejection of punishment—except in extremis and even then in tightly controlled dosages—for sixteen- and seventeen-year-old property offenders.

The Task Force suggests that nonviolent first offenders under eighteen, charged with property felonies should be screened out of our criminal processes *without appearing before a judge,* even a juvenile court judge. But in suggesting that second property offenders and violent offenders in the same age group appear before judges, the Report recognizes that the awesomeness of the judicial processes—rather than virtually automatic administrative sifting—may be so impressive itself to *some* of the young as to have some deterrent impact, quite apart from any punishment. If that is so—and I believe it to be—I should think it also sound to bring this deterrent process into play for young first property offenders.

Many so-called first offenders have in fact previously been subjected to informal *police* release procedures. I do not believe it makes sense to wait until a pattern of criminal conduct has developed before bringing to bear such nonpunitive artillery as may be available to dissuade the young from continued criminality. The finger-in-the-dike may stop the trickle and save the hamlet; it will not serve once the flood has been loosed.

Not only do I think that court (be it juvenile or criminal) rather than administrative processes is sound for young felony offenders, even the first time they are arrested; I also believe that the due process protections that the courts afford are far sounder and far more likely to function in the interests of the accused than is administrative processing. Such processing is done privately (indeed, secretly), is generally subject to the vaguest of standards, and is likely to be conducted by personnel who may lack the special sensitivities and intelligence that we like to think our judges possess. It is increasingly recognized that one of the ills of our criminal justice system is the massive unbridled, unreviewed (and unreviewable) discretion within it: the question of whether witnesses do or do not make complaints; the authority of police to determine whether or not to arrest; and the judgment of prosecutors in terms of bail requests, decisions to prosecute, plea bargaining, and the like. Only now are we starting to see the need for reasonably tight administrative control over these decisions. I believe it sound to discourage administrative decisionmaking and to encourage court action, which is governed by rules and subject to intelligent review. I believe that court proceedings, however ineffectual portions of our judiciary may be, are far more sound, in protecting both society and the rights of defendants, than are procedures that may dispose of felony charges without ever bringing those charges to the light of a courtroom. I also fear the responses of administrative personnel to the fiat of their superiors to "dispose of more cases" as the caseloads build, or to "be tougher" in response to particular journalistic campaigns. With all the weaknesses of our judiciary, I much prefer the courage and independence of the courtroom.

Apart from these general comments about what may be deemed the "philosophy" of the Report, I have made a few specific observations.

The Report suggests that adolescents from fifteen to eighteen might be tried either in juvenile courts or possibly in a "special court for young offenders."* Having noted that choice, and having concluded that individuals in this age group do not belong in criminal court, the Report favors juvenile court jurisdiction. I grant this may be a labeling issue in part. But I do not believe that all offenders through seventeen years of age belong in juvenile court. Seventeen-year-olds are hardly juveniles. I do not know why, within our variegated court systems—particularly in our major urban areas in which the crime problem, alas, is too massive—we cannot recommend the use of special courts, separate from the juvenile faculties, for offenders in this age group.

The Report recommends that the age for criminal court jurisdiction might be lowered for particularly violent crimes, such as murder and rape.** Although I agree as to the soundness of this special concern with violence, there *is* such a thing as aggravated property crime. The Report refers, for example, to "the first arrested vandal, shoplifter, thief, or joyrider."*** I, on the other hand, have in mind the mindless looter and arsonist who may deprive hard-working persons of their life savings; the willful and deliberate "con artist" whose schemes have similar impact and are used against a

*See pp. 8–9.
**See p. 10.
***See p. 13.

series of victims; repetitive patterns of hotel larcenies, warehouse and dock thefts, and the like. I, therefore, must reject a sentencing structure that provides no substantial sanctions for nonviolent crime, however deliberate and repetitive. A maximum of one year's detention and another year of state-imposed lesser sanctions for a *multiply offending* seventeen-year-old "felon" may not, in some circumstances, be adequate to safeguard the community; a maximum sentence of two-and-a-half years for a twenty-year-old multiple offender, similarly, may not be sufficient.*

In contrast, the Task Force's consideration of *violent* youth crimes is sound, in my view. The Report notes the range of opinion within the Task Force in this area, and so dissent is not in order.

---

*Under current legislation, judges may sentence adults who are convicted of property crimes to quite lengthy terms. Were adult sentencing policy to be less stringent, a *proportional* policy for the young would be appropriate.

DISSENT by Marvin E. Wolfgang

There is no compelling or convincing evidence that persons aged sixteen to eighteen differ significantly from persons aged eighteen and over in their capacity to understand the outcomes and consequences of their acts.

I am in favor of reducing sentencing disparity, especially for serious and seriously repetitive offenders, regardless of age. Youth should be given all the aid that helping and educational services can offer. But serious crime should be treated seriously regardless of the offender's age. Neither youth nor old age requires less of a collective response to serious crime than does middle age.

In short, late adolescence is not a meaningful category for criminal offenders. After age sixteen, at least, all persons should be treated by the agents of social control in the same humane ways. Even as adults, offenders are entitled to humane treatment. Humanity, not juveniles or adults, should be the object of concern. All persons, regardless of age, should be given due process and be treated with equality and gentility.

25

Background Paper
by Franklin E. Zimring

This effort is dedicated to Carl and Daniel Zimring, with love and hope for their emerging generation.

Acknowledgments

In preparing this paper, I have had the good fortune to be assisted by an informal advisory committee of three colleagues: Norval Morris, Margaret Rosenheim, and Francis Allen. Their moral and intellectual support enabled me to produce this document. I also have benefited from the reactions of Nina Cobb and Marc Plattner of the Twentieth Century Fund staff, members of the Task Force, and Michael Tonry to an earlier draft of the paper. Brian Forst of the Institute for the Study of Law and Social Policy provided access to the PROMIS data reported in Chapter II. Ellen Fredel provided energetic and intelligent research assistance, and support from the Nancy G. and Raymond G. Feldman Fund at the University of Chicago Law School provided the opportunity to collect much of the data reported in this effort.

Introduction

Every society views its young with a mixture of hope and trepidation. The young are a society's future, for good or ill, and are the focus of special efforts to educate, to protect, and to transmit culture from one generation to the next. Western democracies in general and the United States in particular attempt to nurture and protect their young in an atmosphere of personal freedom and physical mobility, a setting that provides rich opportunities for positive individual growth and almost unlimited potential for deviation from expected social behavior.

Adolescence, the transition from childhood to adulthood, is a period of danger and opportunity. In American culture, adolescence is not strictly associated with physical development or chronological age. As G. H. Elder, Jr., observes:

> Despite a lack of consensus among social scientists on the social boundaries of contemporary adolescence, the clearest marker for entry into adolescence is the transition from primary to secondary school. . . . Entry into one or more adult roles (marriage, parenthood, full-time employment, financial independence) is commonly regarded as the upper boundary.[1]

In American life, adolescents are physically strong before they are emotionally mature, enjoy physical mobility and freedom from supervision before they can make responsible life choices, and have the ability to do serious harm long before they fully realize their capacity to follow the rules and restrictions that society expects adults to obey. It is thus not surprising that youth crime is a growth industry in the United States and that dealing with the youthful offender presents a set of complex and difficult policy issues that can never be resolved in a totally satisfactory manner.

Public policy toward youth crime is inherently ambivalent; society must both protect the young and discourage them from committing crimes. Criminal acts committed by the young are properly seen both as behavior

31

for which the offender is responsible and as a failure on the part of family, society, and the state to discharge their obligations to nurture and to socialize. Criminal acts committed by the young are no less dangerous than those committed by adults; yet state and society have special obligations to youth, including those young persons who have violated the criminal law.

This paper addresses the special problem of dealing with the youthful offender in both juvenile and criminal courts. *The basic assumption is that the policy problems of dealing with youth crime do not change dramatically with the jurisdictional label attached to the young offender.* At present, a young offender's classification as juvenile or adult depends much more on the maximum jurisdictional age set forth in his state's juvenile court act than on the offense he is charged with or the level of his social and emotional growth. The maximum age of juvenile court jurisdiction currently varies from under sixteen in Connecticut, Kentucky, Nebraska, New York, North Carolina, and Vermont to under nineteen in Wyoming. This three-year period itself is of special importance; 41 percent of all arrests for serious crimes of persons under eighteen involve persons over sixteen. Under current law, a sixteen-year-old is a juvenile in Pennsylvania and an adult in New York. But even if all the states reached agreement on a particular age boundary, it is clear that any system that uses a simple "magic birthday" to determine the boundary of youth for purposes of criminal justice policy is arbitrary and in sharp contrast to the insights of developmental psychology and common sense.

The mission of this paper is to examine social policy toward the young offender in both juvenile and criminal courts. The "young offender" discussed in this paper is within the age range that begins with the onset of puberty and continues through adolescence until age twenty-one. The purpose of this definition is not to endorse a judgment that youth ends, for public policy purposes, on an individual's twenty-first birthday but to provide a frame of reference within which to argue that individuals who commit crimes during their adolescent years deserve separate treatment from adults or children and that considering the treatment of these young offenders in the variety of systems that process them will provide a framework for coherent policy.

Chapter I briefly summarizes the types of crimes, types of offenders, and trends in youth crime in the United States.

Chapter II describes the two judicial institutions that process young offenders—the juvenile and criminal courts—and the factors that determine which institution will assume jurisdiction in a particular case.

Chapter III is concerned with the motives that affect dispositional decisions about young offenders.

Chapter IV examines several recent proposals to change sentencing procedures for young offenders. At first glance, the ideological spectrum of the recent crop of reform proposals appears quite broad, ranging from punitive approaches to "radical nonintervention" and its corollary assumption that incarceration is inappropriate for the young offender. In part, however, the apparent divergence in approach reflects attempts to deal with different kinds of cases.

Chapter V surveys options in dispositional policy for specific types of young offenders, ranging from children who engage in activities that are permitted to adults but prohibited to youths through persistent violent offenders.

Limits of the Study

Institutions other than courts—schools, police, social agencies, and correctional agencies—also play important roles in determining what happens to youth. This paper does not deal with these institutions. Moreover, within the court systems examined, the paper does not address in sufficient detail the critical issue of pretrial detention—even though up to ten times as many juveniles as undergo formal post-trial commitment are detained before the adjudication of charges against them.

Coherent theory and coordinated practice are sorely needed in police and correctional policy toward youth crime and in the detention policy of juvenile and criminal courts. A unified perspective, applied to the sanctioning of the young offender, would accomplish little unless it were also applied to the policies of other parts of the system and to determinations as important as detention. My purpose in refraining from detailed considerations of these topics is only to make the Task Force's undertaking manageable. But I would hope that any progress toward a unified jurisprudence of youth crime might affect the formulation of policy throughout the systems that deal with young offenders.

Of course, improvements—however desirable—in these systems cannot be expected to have substantial impact on crime rates. The major determinants of the kinds and quantity of crimes committed by the young lie outside the network of formal legal controls in the larger setting of society. A society that combines nontotalitarian social controls with a permanent, largely minority, urban underclass must expect prodigiously high rates of serious youth criminality. But this expectation provides no excuse for failing to strive toward consistency, coherence, and appropriate balance in sentencing the young offender.

I/ Youth and Crime in American Society

In a series of surveys stretching over the past thirty-five years, the great majority of American young people responding to questions about their own experiences reported having committed crimes. As the National Crime Commission commented in 1966:

> These studies reveal that perhaps 90% of all young people have committed at least one act for which they could have been brought to the juvenile court.[1]

Such findings are sometimes used to support the proposition that "we are all criminals" or to refute figures suggesting relationships between such factors as social class or slum-dwelling and crime. But most of the criminal conduct reported by most of the survey respondents was neither serious nor the beginning of a criminal career. For policy analysis, the difference between the various types of crime is greater than that between criminal and noncriminal behavior. Obviously, some deviation from legal norms is typical, indeed almost universal, in the passage from childhood to adulthood. Just as obviously, of the many young people who violate the law, only a small proportion are consequently brought under social control.

A large proportion of serious crime is reported to and by the police. Most young people who persistently engage in serious crime are apprehended by the police. Official statistics on youth crime and young criminals tell a partial but important story. The arrest statistics in the Uniform Crime Reports prepared each year by the Federal Bureau of Investigation (FBI) indicate that young offenders are responsible for a majority of serious property crimes and a disproportionate share of violent offenses.[2] (See Table I-1.) The amount of crime attributable to the young in the United States is grossly disproportionate to the youth population. In 1975, males between fifteen and twenty years of age represented 8.5 percent of

Table I-1 Percentage of All Arrests Involving Suspects
under 18 and under 21 by Crime. U.S., 1975

	% under 18	% under 21
Homicide	10	25
Rape	18	37
Aggravated Assault	18	32
Robbery	34	58
Burglary	53	73
Larceny	45	63
Auto Theft	55	72
Vandalism	65	78
Drugs	24	53

Source: FBI Uniform Crime Reports. 1975.

the population aged fifteen and over; this group accounted for 45 percent of all FBI Index Crime arrests (violent crimes and most property offenses), 35 percent of all arrests for FBI-classified violent crimes, and 50 percent of all drug law arrests reported by the police.

Estimates based on arrest statistics overstate the role of the young both because younger offenders may be more easily caught than adult offenders and because the young commit their offenses, as they live their lives, in groups. Therefore, they are often arrested in groups for the same crime.[3] Yet the enormous difference in arrest rates cannot be explained by such factors. In large measure, America's crime problem is its youth problem and vice versa.

Offense-Specific Patterns

Middle and late adolescents are disproportionately involved in almost all criminal activity, but the pattern of youth involvement in criminal acts varies with the nature of the crime. Table I-2 depicts this variation by showing the peak age of arrest for each of the Index crimes, the relative "youth-proneness" of each crime type (as measured by the extent to which the arrest rates of youths exceed those of twenty-three-year-olds), and the annual arrest rate per 100,000 of the highest-risk age cohort in the population.

As Table I-2 shows, the peak years for burglary, auto theft, and larceny

Table I-2 Peak Arrest Age, Youth Proneness, and Annual Arrest
Rate per 100,000 Males by Crime, 1975

	Peak Arrest Age	Youth Proneness (Peak Age Arrest Rate/Age 23 Arrest Rate)	Annual Peak Rate of Arrest per 100,000
Homicide	20	1.00	25.4
Rape	18	1.25	41.8
Aggravated Assault	18	1.14	297.0
Robbery	18	1.86	338.2
Burglary	16	3.73	1476.4
Larceny	16	2.81	2407.0
Auto Theft	16	5.21	497.8
Vandalism	15	5.01	497.2
Drugs	18	1.79	1549.2

Sources: FBI Uniform Crime Reports, 1973, and Census Estimates.

occur relatively early in mid-adolescence, and the dropoff between peak rates from mid-adolescence to young adulthood is dramatic. Vandalism, a property crime without pecuniary gain for the offender, is almost the exclusive domain of adolescence. These property crimes and drug offenses account for about nine out of every ten arrests of individuals under age twenty-one.

The pattern for violent offenses is substantially different. Robbery, assault, and rape arrests peak later in adolescence, at age eighteen, and the contrast between youth and young adult rates is far less dramatic for these than for other crimes. Arrests for homicide do not appear to be more concentrated among adolescents than among young adults.

The concentration of crime among the young is both good news and bad news. The good news is that much of the criminal activity attributable to the young seems to abate with age. As they pass from the turbulent years of adolescence to the period of "settling in" that characterizes the early twenties, most young offenders—whether or not they are apprehended and whether or not they participate in official rehabilitation programs—seem to commit fewer offenses. For most adolescents, age alone is the cure for criminality.

The bad news involves those whose criminal behavior age does not cure. Most serious criminal careers begin in the adolescent years.[4] Our capacity to nip criminal careers in the bud is either trivial or nonexistent, depending on which theory one accepts in the heated debate over youth corrections. A small number of youthful offenders will become the next decade's persistent criminals. And despite a number of studies on the subject,[5] our capacity to distinguish those offenders who will outgrow criminal activity from those who will not is limited.

Youth Crime and the Youth Population

Serious youth crime occurs more often in cities than nonurban areas, involves boys far more frequently than girls, and is concentrated—particularly for offenses of violence—among low-social-status, ghetto-dwelling urban youth. The self-report studies convey the impression that youth crime is an adolescent cultural universal, but FBI-collected police statistics indicate that serious youth crime is concentrated among urban minority group males and that the more serious the crime the more pronounced the pattern of concentration.

Table I-3 shows the concentration of crime in large urban areas.

Table I-3 Serious Crime by City Size, U.S., 1975,
by Type of Crime (Arrests per 100,000)

	250,000+ City Size	All Other Areas	Ratio of City/Other
Homicide	21.3	6.7	3.2
Rape	55.5	19.9	2.8
Aggravated Assault	369.0	187.0	2.1
Robbery	678.0	110.0	6.2
Burglary	2368.0	1344.0	1.8
Larceny	3612.0	2690.0	1.3
Auto Theft	1015.0	342.0	3.0

Source: FBI Uniform Crime Reports, 1975.

Offenses of violence are intensely concentrated in the big cities (except for aggravated assault); more common youth offenses are more democratically distributed across demographic borders.

The official delinquency statistics for whole cities do not convey the variations in delinquency rates among communities within cities. Table I-4

Table I-4 Rates[a] of Male Juvenile Delinquents
Selected Chicago Areas, 1966–72

Community Area	Rate
Woodlawn	33.5
South Shore	16.5
Chatham	15.0
Avalon Park	10.6
Calumet Heights	5.9
Chicago Lawn	5.3
West Lawn	3.7
Ashburn	1.7

[a] Rate equals number of males brought before the Juvenile
Court of Cook County on delinquency petitions per 100
males.

Source: Institute for Juvenile Research, Chicago, Illinois.

reports on delinquency rates for eight communities in Chicago.

As the table shows, reported official delinquency rates vary within the city by a factor of almost twenty. The aggregate variables we use in discussing crime, such as city size, hide large variations that exist within the city. The figures for individual communities highlight the weakness of analyses based on such factors as city size, age, sex, race, and social class. Such crude statistics are all we have, but they do not reveal the true concentration of youth crime within categories.

Table I-5 shows that crime is primarily the province of young males. The differences in volume of arrests between males and females, particularly for violent offenses, are dramatic. To some extent, these differences may reflect reluctance on the part of the police to arrest girls or to charge an arrested female with criminal conduct (rather than to place her in an alternative category, such as "minor in need of supervision"). But the persistence and magnitude of the difference between the sexes in crime statistics suggest that this difference is something more than a product of chivalry in the criminal justice system.

In the same vein, the available statistics indicate that urban minority youth are disproportionately involved in serious—particularly violent— crime, although the statistics probably overstate the difference between the races. A number of studies of official statistics, victim survey reports,[6] and

Table I-5   Distribution of Arrests for Persons
Under 18 Years of Age,[a] by Sex and Offense
(Excluding Rape), 1975

	Percentage Male	Percentage Female	Total Arrests
Homicide	90	10	1,373
Robbery	93	7	40,796
Aggravated Assault	84	16	30,858
Burglary	95	5	201,569
Larceny	71	29	378,713
Auto Theft	93	7	56,926
Vandalism	92	8	100,942
Drugs	84	16	103,252

[a] Data not available for 18- to 20-year-olds.
Source: FBI Uniform Crime Reports, 1975.

studies of delinquent careers that support this conclusion[7] also call into question our ability to determine the relative rates of criminal activity of minority and nonminority youth with any accurancy or to disentangle race, class, and official policy as explanations for the wide racial differences observed in aggregate official statistics.

Figure I-1, adapted from a recent study of urban delinquency, reports racial differences for a "birth cohort" of males born in 1945 and followed through official statistics to age eighteen. More recent statistics confirm the differences between races in city arrest rates. Table I-6 illustrates black/ white arrest ratios for four crimes in five American cities for the census year of 1970. These comparisons overstate racial differences because black youths are more frequently arrested in groups than white youths and because of the undercount of the census of the minority youth population.[8] The statistics also obscure differences in social and economic status that account for much of the differential. But the basic pattern—the disproportionate involvement of minority youths in crimes of violence and their less dramatic overrepresentation in property crime—is a fact of modern

Figure I-1 Delinquent Offenders in Philadelphia by Frequency Category and Race, Males Only

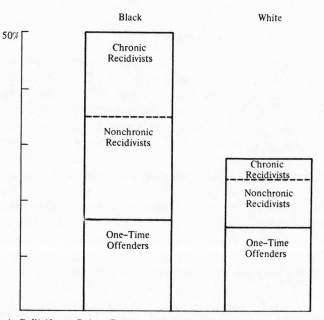

Table I-6 Ratio of Black to White Arrest Rates, per 100,000
Youths by Crime in Five Cities[a] (1970)

Homicide	7.2
Robbery	8.6
Burglary	3.9
Auto Theft	3.0

[a] Boston, Chicago, Cleveland, Dallas, Washington, D.C.

Source: Franklin Zimring, "Crime, Demography and Time in
Five American Cities" (paper prepared for the Hudson Institute)

urban life and a necessary partial explanation for recent trends in youth crime.

Recent Trends

The fifteen years from 1960 to 1975 were characterized by three demographic shifts that constitute an ideal prescription for explosive increases in youth crime: a large increase in the youth population, an increased concentration of the young in urban areas, and a huge increase in the minority youth population in core cities. These population changes occurred in a social setting where crime rates for all significant age groups were increasing. Given generally higher crime rates as well as large increases in the population-at-risk, a substantial increase in youth crime was predictable.

Table I-7 compares volume of arrests for 1960 with volume of arrests for 1975. The increase in arrests was smaller than the increase in crimes committed during this period;[9] the number of arrests per hundred crimes fell significantly. At the same time, the youth population increased dramatically. The figures in Table I-7 are not adjusted to reflect either the ratio of crimes to arrests or the ratio of youth population to crimes committed.

Table 1-7 Arrests by Crime, Ages 13–20, 1960 and 1975

	1960	1975	Percentage Increase
Homicide	973	4,149	326
Rape	3,064	8,137	165
Robbery	15,141	74,903	394
Aggravated Assault	12,342	65,316	429
Burglary	89,175	325,970	265
Larceny	141,897	602,132	324
Auto Theft	44,038	87,843	99
Vandalism	a	137,154	
Drugs	9,935	269,202	2609

[a] Vandalism data not reported in 1960; no increase can be calculated for the 1960–75 time span.

Source: FBI Uniform Crime Reports, 1960 and 1975.

Given these shifts, the table overstates the growth in youth crime. However, the volume of arrests is an appropriate beginning for any analysis of official responses to crime because it is the arrest rather than the crime that activates the decisional process.

From 1960 to 1975, the volume of "part I" arrests of offenders under twenty-one for FBI Index Crimes increased from 300,000 to more than 1 million. And the most serious offenses, notably, robbery, homicide, and assault, experienced the most substantial percentage increases.[10]

A number of trends in youth crime arrests over the past few years deserve special attention. Arrests of female offenders for serious offenses have increased more substantially than arrests of males. The extent to which this change reflects "relabeling" rather than a real increase in criminality among young women is unknown. With the exception of larceny, which includes shoplifting, differences in arrest statistics between the sexes remain and seem likely to continue to be vast.[11]

Of greater importance is the shift of juvenile arrests from city to suburbs. The youth population of the United States is shifting from city to suburb. Those crimes that are especially concentrated in adolescent groups, particularly Index property crime and the youth-dominated crimes of vandalism and drug offenses, seem to be following the migration to the suburbs, while offenses of violence remain in the city, concentrated among males and the minority poor.[12] Arrests for violent offenses may yet become more evenly distributed among the youth population, but they are far more likely to remain concentrated within the residual youth population of 250,000 and over.

Implications for Reform

Youth crime is not a unitary phenomenon; it is a label that encompasses a wide variety of events with different consequences and different implications for sentencing. The volume and variety of youth criminality argue against any single rigid dispositional policy toward the young offender. High volume and hard choices will confront any set of social institutions that respond to youth crime and the young offender. There is little doubt that law and policy need to be reformed. But intelligent reform proposals must be grounded in the facts about youth crime.

II / Our Dual System of Justice for Young Offenders

Like most crime control policy in the United States, youth crime policy is the responsibility of state and local governments and varies substantially from state to state. But every state (as well as the District of Columbia) has a juvenile or family court responsible for handling some young offenders and a criminal court responsible for handling the remainder. Where a particular offender will come to rest in this dual system depends, first, on the particular state's legislative definition of the "jurisdictional age" that marks the border between juvenile and criminal courts and, second, on the discretion available to prosecutors and courts to "waive" individuals whose age would otherwise qualify them for the juvenile court's jurisdiction.

A sixteen-year-old who is accused of robbery in New York will be processed by the criminal court because, under that state's family court legislation, the offender's sixteenth birthday marks the boundary between family court and criminal court.[1] A sixteen-year-old who is accused of robbery in Pennsylvania will be processed in the juvenile court, whose jurisdiction extends, as it does in most states, to the eighteenth birthday,[2] unless the juvenile court exercises its discretion to "waive" jurisdiction over the offender and thus sends him to the criminal court. Most states have laws that provide for such waivers;[3] few states provide any explicit criteria on which to base the waiver decision.[4] Figure II-1 shows the maximum ages for juvenile court jurisdiction in the fifty states and the District of Columbia.

Jurisdictional age varies from under sixteen to under nineteen; the largest number of jurisdictions reserve the juvenile court for persons who have not yet reached eighteen. The issue of what age is appropriate for juvenile court jurisdiction is constantly before state legislatures. Between 1972 and 1977, ten states changed the age for delinquency jurisdiction.[5] Six of these states raised the maximum jurisdictional age to the national

45

Figure II-1 Maximum for Delinquency Jurisdiction in Juvenile Courts: 1977

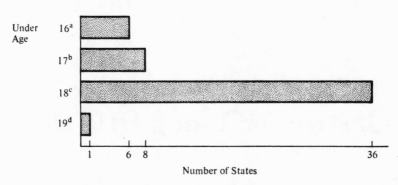

Number of States

Source: National Center for State Courts

[a] Conn., Ky., Nebr., N.Y., N.C., Vt.
[b] Ga., Ill., La., Mass., Mich., Mo., S.C., Tex.
[c] Ala., Alaska, Ariz., Ark., Calif., Colo., Del., D.C., Hawaii, Idaho,
   Ind., Iowa, Kans., Maine, Md., Minn., Miss., Mont., Nev., N.H., N.J., N. Mex.,
   N. Dak., Ohio, Okla., Oreg., Pa., R.I., S. Dak., Tenn., Utah, Va., Wash., W. Va., Wis.
[d] Wyo.

norm of eighteen. One state increased the age to nineteen. One lowered it to
seventeen, and two lowered it to sixteen.[6] Almost all reform standards call
for jurisdiction until age eighteen.[7]

The Juvenile Court and the Treatment of Delinquency

The policy of treating age as a relevant criterion in assessing criminal
liability has a substantial history. Under common law, children under the
age of seven were deemed incapable of committing criminal acts; the
capacity of any child under fourteen had to be proved as an element of the
Crown's case in any criminal proceeding.[8] In the United States in the nine-
teenth century, a number of other special provisions for treatment of young
offenders were the precursors of the juvenile court movement.[9]

The first juvenile court was established in Illinois in 1899; it represented a quantum jump in the jurisprudence of youth crime.[10] As Judge
Julian Mack described it, the criminal law was inappropriate for juveniles
because:

> It put one question, "Has he committed this crime?" It did not inquire,
> "What is the best to do for this lad?" . . . [T]he punishment was visited in pro-
> portion to the degree of wrongdoing evidenced by the single act; not by the
> needs of the boy; not by the needs of the state.[11]

The juvenile court, in contrast, was to act as a substitute parent for the young offender, as well as for other children in trouble. The subject matter of the court was children in need of help or supervision, as well as those adults who caused or contributed to the need for intervention.

Those who founded the juvenile court rejected the concept of punishing young minors for criminal offenses. A minor who had committed an offense was not to be considered a criminal, and the juvenile court's response to the offense was not to be punitive.[12]

In assuming power over the life of a child, the court would simply seek to meet the child's need for help. The child's behavior was of interest to the juvenile court purely as a sign that intervention was needed; the degree of intervention would depend on the child's need for reform and guidance.

The court had power to determine whether a child under its jurisdiction was neglected, dependent, or delinquent. Neglect was generally defined as the result of culpable parental failure to provide necessary care, while dependency was a category that reflected the child's need for care independent of fault and often involved children without parents.[13] The definition of delinquency was typically quite broad. As the President's Crime Commission commented in 1966:

> [T]he definition of conduct making one eligible for the category of delinquency was not limited by conduct criminal for adults but rather amounted virtually to a manual of undesirable youthful behavior.... The juvenile court also undertook to reenforce the duties owed parents and schools by children. Thus truancy was included among the bases for ... jurisdiction, as was the catch-all state variously called incorrigibility, ungovernability, uncontrolability, or simply "beyond control."[14]

The justification of the breadth of this definition was the protective and rehabilitative motives of the juvenile court and a concept of social justice that called forth "new efforts to bring law out of isolation and into partnership with the ascending social and behavioral sciences."[15] The juvenile court's purpose was to help, and the broader the definition of delinquency, the larger the number of children it would qualify for such help. The court's purpose was not to punish; hence, the court did not need to distinguish between criminal and noncriminal acts in assigning delinquent status to young people under its jurisdiction. The state's purpose for intervening was to benefit these young people; hence, the court did not need to justify the amount of intervention in terms of proportionality to the harm the minor had done. These assumptions, which have dominated juvenile justice for most of the last century, comprise what I shall refer to as the "omnibus theory of delinquency."

In contrast to the criminal law, this theory of juvenile justice does not vary according to whether or not a young person has violated the law or with the severity of that violation. Criminal justice as theoretically applied to adult offenders categorizes crimes and assigns punishments that vary with the nature and severity of the offense. The omnibus theory of delinquency, in contrast, categorizes all undesirable youthful behavior as delinquent, rejecting the notion that the state's response should be keyed to an actual violation of the law or proportional to the severity of that violation.

In the three-quarters of a century since its inception, the basic jurisprudential notions and nomenclature of the juvenile court have undergone surprisingly few changes. Some states have carried the juvenile court into the larger framework of a family court that undertakes comprehensive supervision of the legal aspects of the family and the legal meanings of childhood.[16] Many states have restricted the assignment of delinquent status to children who have committed acts in violation of the penal law, but most of these states have retained power to intervene in the lives of truants and runaways by placing them in another jurisdictional category—"minors in need of supervision" or "children in need of supervision."[17]

From the beginning, the procedural style of the juvenile court has been deliberately informal. The procedural protections designed for defendants in criminal proceedings were considered unnecessary and counterproductive in a court whose mission was child-saving. The juvenile court emphasized treating the child in his community setting. For the most part, this treatment took the form of probation, and probation was the modal disposition for adjudicated delinquents in Illinois as early as 1905, although a substantial number of delinquents were sent to state institutions.[18]

Although in 1967, *In Re Gault* extended due process guarantees for formal adjudications of delinquency, today most delinquency referrals are handled informally,[19] and probation continues to be the standard disposition for offenders who are formally adjudicated delinquent.[20] In most jurisdictions, proceedings are private, and juvenile court records are protected to some extent from public scrutiny.[21]

Although the basic premises and processes of the juvenile court have not changed radically, attitudes about the court have shifted from hope to skepticism. Paternalism, informality, and discretion are frequently viewed as invitations to abuse. The court's treatment of "delinquency" has been attacked as the use of a false label by a system that is both punitive and ineffective. The efficacy of probation has been called into question, and the use of secure juvenile correctional facilities in the name of child-saving has been sharply criticized. At the same time, the juvenile court and juvenile corrections have been accused of undue leniency in the treatment of young offenders.

Beneath these divergent criticisms is a well-founded consensus that the juvenile court's practices do not conform perfectly to the omnibus theory of delinquency and that the court should be judged not on the basis of its announced theories but rather on its actual performance as a youth-processing institution.

Both critics and defenders of the court frequently rest their arguments on value judgments and anecdote; the volume of discussion and debate about the system is far in excess of the reliable empirical data needed for a sound analysis of the court as an institution. The discussion that follows is an attempt to improve the quality of debate on juvenile justice by providing some basic data on young offenders in the juvenile courts of the United States and to relate these data to the courts' dispositional policies.

The Juvenile Court in the 1970s

Figure II-2 presents rough estimates of the number of juveniles arrested, formally referred (the technical term is "petitioned") to the juvenile court, placed on probation, and placed in juvenile correctional facilities in 1973. Clearly, the juvenile justice system is a major industry: 1.3 million arrests, resulting in 500,000 court "intakes" each year; 200,000 young persons under formal social control, 46,000 of these in institutions as a result of dispositional decisions.[22]

Figure II-2 Processing of Arrested Juveniles by Sex, 1973

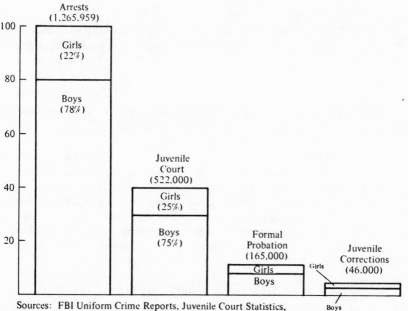

Sources: FBI Uniform Crime Reports, Juvenile Court Statistics,
Juvenile Detention and Correctional Facility Census.

Behind this statistical profile is a complex discretionary system for screening young offenders, particularly in major urban areas. Figure II-3, adapted from the 1966 Crime Commission report, depicts the basic structure of the juvenile justice system. The diagram, although thin on detail, provides a basis for discussion of how the system allocates power among police, intake workers, judges, and correctional agencies. The *police* have the important discretionary decision of whether or not to arrest. It has been estimated that in four out of five incidents, police officers do not arrest eligible juvenile offenders, although the proportion probably varies according to the severity of the offense.[23]

The *intake worker* in urban court systems is typically a probation officer who negotiates with the arresting officer to decide whether or not a petition should be filed alleging that the child is delinquent. If they decide not to file a petition, the case is not technically before the court; arrests that do not result in petitions are referred to as having been handled on an "informal" basis. If a petition is filed, the case is then "formally" or "judicially" handled. Nationwide, about half of all arrests result in the filing of petitions.[24] The petition may then be continued, be dismissed, or lead to what is called an *adjudicatory hearing*—a proceeding in which the factual basis for the petition must be proved through the presentation of evidence or confirmed by the child. At the conclusion of the adjudicatory hearing, the court decides whether or not the minor is "delinquent." If the minor is found to be delinquent, the court holds a *dispositional* hearing to determine what should happen to the delinquent.[25]

These procedures may consume a considerable amount of time. Meanwhile, the minor may be formally detained, returned to his home, or placed elsewhere pending the disposition of the case. Typically, the police have the power to detain juveniles for short periods of time; longer term detention usually requires a hearing held by a judge.[26] The legal criteria for the detention decision range from judicial discretion to relatively detailed statutory directions, such as those provided in Illinois:

> If the court finds that it is a matter of immediate and urgent necessity for the protection of the minor or of the person or property of another that the minor be detained or placed in a shelter care facility or that he is likely to flee the jurisdiction of the court, it may prescribe detention or shelter care and order that the minor be kept in a suitable place designated by the court or in a shelter care facility designated by the Department of Children and Family Services or a licensed child welfare agency; otherwise it shall release the minor from custody.[27]

On any given day, about 11,000 minors are held in secure detention, that is to say, under lock and key. On the average, detained minors are held about ten days. But the duration of detention varies substantially. Each

Figure II-3 A General View of the Juvenile Justice System

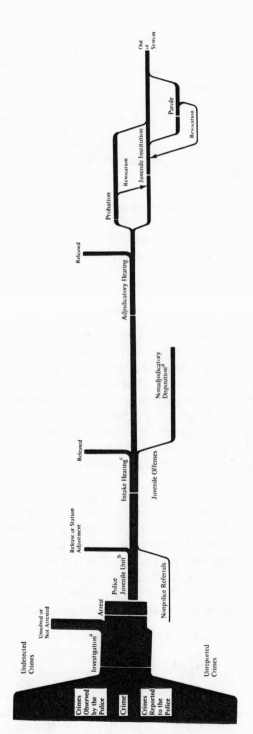

Source: *The Challenge of Crime in a Free Society* (1967), pp. 8–9.

[a] May continue until trial.

[b] Police often hold informal hearing, dismiss, or adjust many cases without further processing.

[c] Probation officer decides desirability of further court action.

[d] Welfare agency, social services, counseling, medical care, etc., for cases where adjudicatory handling not needed.

year, about 400,000 minors are detained before trial, eight times as many as are sent to secure facilities after a dispositional hearing.[28]

The size of the youth crime problem has been suggested as the reason for continued emphasis on informality:

> Sheer volume guarantees that in delinquency cases, the system is a filter where, of every five hundred possible juvenile arrests, it is estimated that there are two hundred police contacts resulting in 100 arrests. Of these, only 40 youths are taken in, only twenty appear before a judge, and only 2 or 3 are sent to a correctional facility.[29]

In fact, this informality is not solely a response to case volume. It also may reflect variations in style among juvenile courts and the preferences of court personnel for informal and low-visibility procedures.[30] The choice of formal or informal disposition leads to different dispositional policy options.

Informal Proceedings

A nationwide sample of juvenile courts reports that more than half of all cases are disposed of without petition.[31] Many observers believe that this informality is preferable, from the perspective of the child's welfare, to the stigma of formal court processing.[32] When a juvenile arrest is handled informally, the dispositional alternatives available to the court worker are limited. The intake officer may refer the youth to another social agency, relying on the voluntary cooperation of the youth and his family or on the continued threat of formal prosecution to make the referral effective. In many other cases, the intake officer merely delivers a warning or admonition to the young offender.[33]

Another dispositional alternative for informally handled cases is a structured pretrial division and treatment program, but such programs are not widely available and it is difficult to estimate with any reliability the extent of participation in them or the proportion of informally processed young offenders who reach such programs.[34] The one punitive disposition available for informally processed offenders is temporary detention.[35] The number of punitive pretrial detentions is substantial, but specific data on the combination of informal processing and short-term detention are not currently available.

Formal Proceedings

A "formally" processed juvenile is not necessarily one who has the merits of the charges against him determined by a juvenile court judge[36] but merely one who remains in the system after undergoing the intake screening process of the juvenile court. The juvenile court judge decides whether his case will be continued, dismissed,[37] or subject to an adjudicatory hearing to establish whether or not the juvenile is within one of the jurisdictional categories of the court.[38]

If an offender is adjudicated to be a child or minor in need of supervision, he may be placed on probation or in a nonsecure residential custodial setting. Many recent statutes establishing this subdelinquent category for juveniles under the court's jurisdiction prohibit the placement of such children in secure correctional institutions after but not before adjudication of the charges against them.[39]

In the dispositional hearing that typically follows the adjudication of a juvenile as delinquent, the options available to the judge include:

1.   no action

2.   informal supervision

3.   a formal order of probation

4.   a variety of placements to public and private agencies providing counseling, residential care in group homes, or foster care

5.   commitment to a state institution for an indeterminate period of time not to exceed whatever age is specified in that state's juvenile court legislation.[40]

As a result of *Gault* and subsequent cases, a child can demand representation at the adjudication and perhaps at the dispositional hearing on delinquency charges.[41] But the dispositional decision is discretionary; the opinion of the individual judge is the determining factor in nearly all cases. Thus, in an important sense, the Constitution may provide the delinquent with a lawyer but not with a rule of law to govern his fate in the dispositional hearing.

Formal probation varies in intensity from occasional visits to a probation officer to close supervision with specific conditions. Placement with a public or private agency varies from community supervision to foster care or to a residential institution.[42] Commitment to a juvenile institution is typically indeterminate; the correctional authority rather than the judge determines the time a young offender will serve. In theory, a sixteen-year-old may serve as much as five years in a juvenile institution before release for a trivial offense. In practice, in 1973 the average stay in a juvenile institution was estimated at 8.7 months.[43]

Diversion and Due Process

Most of those who accuse the juvenile court of over-intervention in the lives of young offenders argue that formal court processing, regardless of the outcome, harms those who are subjected to it. Some observers also argue that adult defendants, too, suffer from the stigma or "labeling" effect of criminal court processing. As a response to these criticisms, a number of "pretrial diversion" programs have been introduced, placing low-risk offenders in various treatment and helping programs and keeping them out of the formal system.[44] Some defendants may indeed be better off staying out of court. To divert, by definition, is to avoid the formal determination that results in the negative label. But diversion programs also put the state in the position of intervening in the lives of persons who might be found innocent if passed on in the system.

Two proposed solutions to this problem illustrate the conflict between diversion and due process. One approach involves restricting admission to such programs to persons who acknowledge, in writing, their "factual guilt."[45] How a program explicitly devoted to the "factually guilty" helps avoid stigma and labeling is hard to fathom. Nor can such a procedure be trusted to screen out the innocent; anyone who fears the consequences of formal involvement may choose to sign such a paper. The proposal serves only to benefit those defendants who do not insist on their innocence.

Another approach involves holding a due process hearing on guilt or innocence before diverting a defendant into a treatment program. This arrangement serves to limit the extent to which coercive state power may be invoked without a hearing,[46] but it also subjects the defendant to a form of criminal justice processing, however streamlined, and imposes a pejorative label of some sort on him before he can be diverted. Moreover, because it would increase the time taken by each formal diversion, such a requirement would tend to discourage court and prosecutor from using the diversion approach and encourage them to dispose of more defendants prior to the due process hearing.

The diversion movement of the past decade, with its emphasis on using informal helping and treatment programs and avoiding the stigma of social condemnation, shares many of the goals and problems of Judge Mack's ideal of the juvenile court.[47] There is some irony in the efforts of modern reformers to save young offenders from the stigma of the court he thought would preclude stigma. Even more troublesome is the possibility that the machinery of pretrial diversion could itself come to resemble the juvenile court the reformers are trying to avoid.

Determinants of Disposition in the Juvenile Court

Juvenile court legislation provides little guidance to the legal principles and decisional processes that determine where a particular juvenile will "end up" in the system. Some states prohibit secure custody for children "in need of supervision," and a few prohibit such custody for "status offenders"[48]—those whose offenses are not violations of criminal law. But the bulk of the court caseload is other types of delinquents; most systems leave the decision on disposition of children who have committed offenses to the discretion of the court, and commitments to juvenile institutions are indeterminate. The omnibus theory of delinquency places less emphasis on the distinctions between various categories of delinquency than between delinquents and nondelinquents and justifies the state's coercive intervention not for what a child does but for what he is. Generally, all adjudicated delinquents face the same range of possible responses and the same maximum sanctions. Discretion, not unknown to adult criminal processes, is the dominant standard for disposition in the juvenile court.[49]

Waiver—The Transition from Juvenile to Adult Court Jurisdiction

In forty-eight of the fifty states, some accused juveniles may be transferred, or "waived," to the criminal courts in some circumstances. Waiver is a discretionary decision of the juvenile court that usually depends on the seriousness of the individual offense. In some states, prosecutorial discretion or statutes requiring that minors accused of certain crimes be tried in criminal court perform the same function as waiver.[50]

Despite its child-saving mission, the juvenile court early accepted the proposition that some children are beyond salvation. In 1903, the Illinois juvenile probation service was complaining of the need for longer sentences of incarceration for some juveniles, and the court for children was binding fourteen children a year over to the grand jury for criminal proceedings.[51] Today, in most major metropolitan areas, only a tiny percentage of all accused juvenile offenders are waived to the jurisdiction of the criminal courts.[52] In Philadelphia, for example, according to unpublished studies, fewer than 2 percent of robbery arrests and less than half of all arrests for criminal homicide are waived from the juvenile to the adult court.[53]

A body of legal principles, generally accorded constitutional significance, governs the waiver procedure but not the decision itself. In 1966, the factors to be considered by a juvenile court judge in the District of Columbia in making the waiver decision were listed as an appendix to *Kent v. United States,*[54] the leading constitutional case that established procedural safeguards for waiver hearings:

1. The seriousness of the alleged offense to the community and whether the protection of the community requires waiver.

2. Whether the alleged offense was committed in an aggressive, violent, premeditated or willful manner.

3. Whether the alleged offense was against persons or against property, greater weight being given to offenses against persons especially if personal injury resulted.

4. The prosecutive merit of the complaint, i.e., whether there is evidence upon which a Grand Jury may be expected to return an indictment (to be determined by consultation with the United States Attorney).

5. The desirability of trial and disposition of the entire offense in one court when the juvenile's associates in the alleged offense are adults who will be charged with a crime in the U.S. District Court for the District of Columbia.

6. The sophistication and maturity of the juvenile as determined by consideration of his home, environmental situation, emotional attitude and pattern of living.

7. The record and previous history of the juvenile, including previous contacts with the Youth Aid Division, other law enforcement agencies, juvenile courts and other jurisdictions, prior periods of probation to this Court, or prior commitments to juvenile institutions.

8. The prospects for adequate protection of the public and the likelihood of reasonable rehabilitation of the juvenile (if he is found to have committed the alleged offense) by the use of procedures, services and facilities currently available to the Juvenile Court.[55]

These standards are problematic both individually and collectively. For example, the "prosecutive merit" standard (#4) suggests that delinquency should be more easily proved than crime, a frightening proposition, which, in 1970, was held to be unconstitutional.[56] The administrative convenience standard (#5) seems opposed to any principled reason for treating young offenders differently from adult offenders. The "previous contacts" standard (#7) implies that we know when a youth is beyond redemption, and the "sophistication" standard (#6) also involves more guesswork than social science. All of these standards are attacks on the omnibus theory of delinquency; only #1, #2, #3, and #8, deal with social needs for punishment, and #8, which necessarily involves prediction of individual dangerousness, is empirically suspect.[57]

Collectively, "lists" of this length rarely serve to limit discretion or regularize procedure. By giving emphasis to one or two of the guidelines, a judge can usually justify a decision either way. Waiver is an important element of dispositional policy for young offenders; a juvenile charged with an extremely serious offense, such as homicide or robbery, has more of his lifetime at stake in the waiver hearing than at any other stage in the criminal justice process.[58]

In principle, waiver is a denial of both the omnibus theory of delinquency and the rights of children to special protection. But even in states with high juvenile court jurisdictional age limits, very few juveniles are waived into the criminal courts. Legislatively lowering the maximum age by one year would probably draw more young offenders into any court system in any state of the Union than would a discretionary waiver provision. However, if the waiver procedure is to be maintained, it is badly in need of both due process procedural protections and decisional standards. The waiver of juvenile court jurisdiction requires a central guiding principle and judicial scrutiny of waivers at both the trial and appellate levels.

Young Offenders in Criminal Courts

The juvenile court is a discrete institution that has attracted scholars to study its operations in some detail. The careers of young offenders in criminal courts have received much less attention. In most states, the young offender who "ages out" of the juvenile justice system encounters what appears to be a totally different system of decisional principles. Potential criminal liability is determined by the legislatively prescribed maximum sentence for the specific criminal charge. Procedures are formal, and sentences meted out to young offenders can be the same as for other offenders. The process is "offense centered" rather than "child centered," although the sentences may be "individualized" to the particular circumstances of the offender.

Figure II-4 shows the system of formal processing that confronts the youth who has been waived to the criminal court or has passed the maximum age of juvenile court jurisdiction. The chart shows the "law-book" theory of procedure in criminal courts—what can happen as opposed to what does happen in the average case:

> When an infraction of the law occurs, a policeman finds, if he can, the probable offender, arrests him and brings him promptly before a magistrate. If the offense is minor, the magistrate disposes of it forthwith; if it is serious, he holds the defendant for further action and admits him to bail. The case then is turned over to a prosecuting attorney, who charges the defendant with a specific statutory crime. This charge is subject to review by a judge at a preliminary hearing of the evidence and in many places, if the offense charged is a felony, by a grand jury that can dismiss the charge, or affirm it by delivering it to a judge in the form of an indictment. If the defendant pleads "not guilty" to the charge he comes to trial; the facts of his case are marshaled by the prosecuting and defense attorneys and presented, under the supervision of a judge, through witnesses, to a jury. If the jury finds the defendant guilty, he is sentenced by the judge. . . .[59]

The formal processes of the criminal court differ in several respects from those of the juvenile court. The young offender in criminal court is entitled

Figure II-4 A General View of the Criminal Justice System

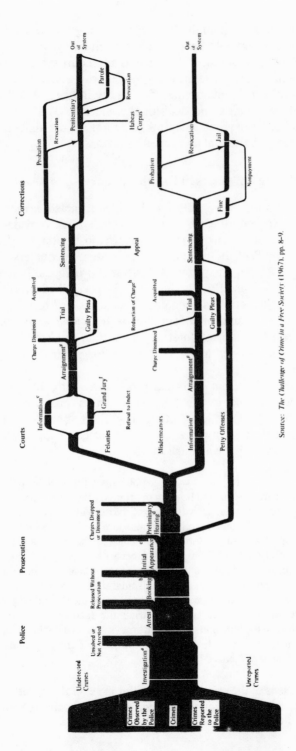

Source: *The Challenge of Crime in a Free Society* (1967). pp. 8-9.

[a] May continue until trial.

[b] Administrative record of arrest. First step at which temporary release on bail may be available.

[c] Before magistrate, commissioner, or justice of peace. Formal notice of charge, advice of rights. Bail set. Summary trials for petty offenses usually conducted here without further processing.

[d] Preliminary testing of evidence against defendant. Charge may be reduced. No separate preliminary hearing for misdemeanors in some systems.

[e] Charge filed by prosecutor on basis of information submitted by police or citizens. Alternative to grand jury indictment: often used in felonies, almost always in misdemeanors.

[f] Reviews whether government evidence sufficient to justify trial. Some states have no grand jury system; others seldom use it.

[g] Appearance for plea; defendant elects trial by judge or jury (if available); counsel for indigent usually appointed here in felonies. Often not at all in other cases.

[h] Charge may be reduced at any time prior to trial in return for plea of guilty or for other reasons.

[i] Challenge on constitutional grounds to legality of detention. May be sought at any point in process.

to bail, a deposit of money as security for his appearance in court, payment of which enables him to avoid pretrial detention. Most states do not provide juveniles with the right to bail. However, criminal court judges often deliberately set money bail at levels beyond the ordinary criminal defendant's capacity to pay;[60] this discretion to set bail is analogous to the discretion that juvenile court judges often have to order prolonged periods of pretrial detention.

The adult defendant, unlike the individual charged with delinquency in the juvenile court, is legally entitled to a jury trial. But probably no more than one out of twenty charges in major metropolitan criminal courts is disposed of by jury trial.[61] It is possible that the right to jury trial influences the behavior of prosecutors and judges in a large number of cases.[62] However, the differences between defendants' rights in juvenile court and defendants' rights in criminal court are greater in theory than in practice. High levels of "case mortality," extensive waiver of constitutional rights, and widespread use of pretrial detention characterize both systems. Under both systems, relatively few people are sentenced to secure post-trial incarceration. But the criminal court can and does sentence convicted offenders to much longer terms of incarceration than the juvenile court.[63] Most authorized sentences of imprisonment in state criminal courts are in excess of the maximum dispositional authority of the juvenile courts.[64] The difference in application between the sentencing policies of juvenile and criminal courts is difficult to measure because sentencing in the adult court is almost always discretionary with the court.

It appears, however, that, because of their age and the protections accorded juvenile court records, younger offenders receive more lenient treatment than older offenders in criminal courts. Figures II-5 and II-6 contrast the age of offenders eighteen and over at arrest with the age-specific rate at which offenders are sent to prison for robbery and larceny.

The data on which these figures are based are flawed in a number of ways. First, the statistics, taken from the Uniform Crime Reports and National Prisoner Statistics for 1972, are aggregated national estimates. Second, they are not adjusted to account for differences in the prior records of offenders. Third, they do not account for the time lag between age at arrest and age at prison admission. Still, the national figures show a pattern in which the ratio of robbery prison admissions to arrests for twenty-three-year-olds is two and a half times as high as for nineteen-year-olds, even though the time lag and high eighteen-year-old arrest rates should place the nineteen-year-old group at a disadvantage. If these figures are representative of reality, youth is a mitigating factor in sentencing policy at least through an offender's twenty-first birthday.

Tables II-1 and II-2 analyze the impact of a young offender's age on the chance he will be convicted in a criminal court, the probability given conviction that he will be incarcerated, and the probability given incarceration

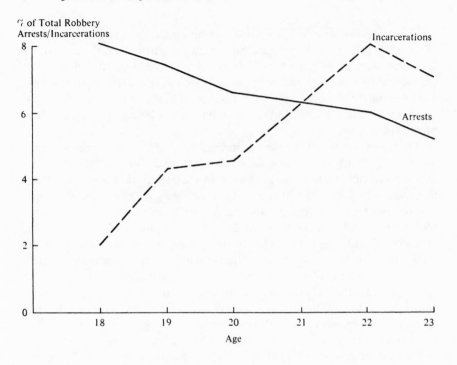

Figure II-5 Percentages of Total Arrests and Incarcerations for Robbery by Age, 1972

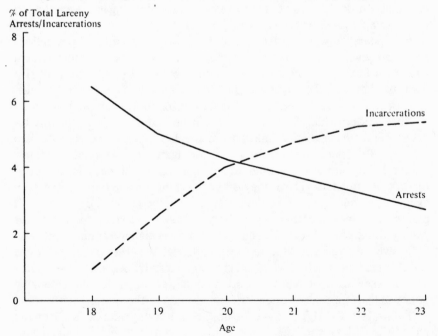

Figure II-6 Percentages of Total Arrests and Incarcerations for Larceny by Age, 1972

that the minimum sentence of the court will be one year or more. The data, collected from case dispositions in the District of Columbia, in 1974, were produced with the cooperation of the Institute for the Study of Law and Social Research.[65]

Table II-1 shows some fluctuation in the percentage of convictions among the various age groups, but no systematic variation with the offender's age. The youngest age group in the sample, eighteen-year-olds, experienced higher than average conviction percentages for both armed robbery and burglary, and the only offense for which young offenders had

Table II-1 Disposition of Persons Accused of Robbery and Burglary by Charge and Age at Arrest, Washington, D. C., 1974

	18	19	20	21	22	23	24	25+	All Ages	Total Cases
% Convicted of Any Charge										
Armed Robbery	33	27	28	33	28	34	27	30	30.5	(969)
Burglary	48	49	43	21	45	46	36	41	42.5	(1472)
% Serving Time of Those Convicted										
Armed Robbery	55	58	79	89	79	61	68	67	66	(196)
Burglary	35	49	45	49	44	47	59	49	49	(625)

even a slightly lower conviction rate than older offenders was robbery. (Somewhat more interesting, the general conviction rate for burglary is substantially higher than that for armed robbery.)

The data on the percentage of convicted offenders serving time do support the hypothesis that younger offenders are treated more leniently but not to the extent that Figures II-5 and II-6 suggest. Only about a third of all convicted eighteen-year-olds originally charged with burglary serve some time; slightly over half of older burglars are incarcerated. Of those convicted of armed robbery, 55 percent of eighteen-year-olds and 58 percent of nineteen-year-olds serve some time. Convicted armed robbers aged twenty through twenty-eight run, on the average, more than an eight-out-of-ten risk of incarceration.

Table II-2 provides data on the minimum sentence imposed by the court for those individuals sentenced to periods of incarceration in the Washington sample. Because under the Federal Youth Corrections Act the District of Columbia courts can provide indeterminate sentences for young offenders, the data in the table are divided into three categories: minimum sentences of less than one year, more than one year, and the indeterminate commitment that is mandated under the Youth Corrections Act.

Table II-2 Minimum Sentence by Age, Armed Robbery, Robbery, and Burglary Suspects Given Custodial Sentences (District of Columbia, 1974)

Age	Less than 1 Year	1 Year or More	Indeterminate	Total
Armed Robbery				
18	---	23	76	100 (17)
19	---	7	93	100 (15)
20	---	35	65	100 (23)
21	---	65	35	100 (23)
22	5	68	26	100 (19)
23	7	93	---	100 (14)
24	13	87	---	100 (15)
25 & over	10	86	3	100 (57)
Robbery				
18	6	17	78	100 (36)
19	6	11	83	100 (35)
20	2	27	70	100 (40)
21	5	61	33	100 (39)
22	3	72	24	100 (29)
23	16	84	---	100 (31)
24	17	83	---	100 (29)
25 & over	20	78	2	100 (112)
Burglary				
18	---	25	75	100 (16)
19	3	8	90	100 (39)
20	27	9	64	100 (22)
21	4	41	54	100 (22)
22	10	80	10	100 (20)
23	37	50	12	100 (24)
24	10	85	5	100 (20)
25 & over	23	66	11	100 (134)

As the table shows, in the District of Columbia age at arrest significantly influences sentence selection. In all three crime categories, most offenders aged twenty and under when arrested are sentenced to indeterminate terms under the Youth Corrections Act, while most older offenders receive minimum sentences of one year or more. The practical impact of this difference in pattern is difficult to estimate because the Youth Corrections Act provides a maximum sentence of four years.[66] Data are not available on the time actually served by the offenders in the sample. But statistics collected previously by the Federal Bureau of Prisons suggest that persons sentenced for burglary under the Youth Corrections Act serve about as much time, on the average, as other burglars committed to the federal prison system.[67] Young robbers committed under the act serve substantially shorter sentences, on the average, than other robbers incarcerated in federal prisons; they benefit from the four-year maximum imposed by the act.[68] The special dispositional policy in the federal courts toward young offenders thus partakes of two characteristics of juvenile court dispositional policy: indeterminacy and sentences less clearly determined by the seriousness of the offense than in sentencing for older offenders.[69]

Although the Washington data provide a clearer and more accurate picture than the earlier national aggregated data, they are not without faults. The tables cover only two offenses in only one jurisdiction. They do not list "prior criminal record" as an independent determinant of the type of sentence or the length of sentence because the juvenile court's jurisdictional age boundary is the eighteenth birthday, and contact with the law prior to that birthday is usually not considered a prior criminal record for sentencing purposes in criminal court.

The Washington data suggest that in the criminal court the seriousness of the offense is the primary determinant of the severity of the sentence but that youth, at least through the first two years of criminal court jurisdiction, is a perceptible mitigating factor. Youth also influences the mode of sentencing because the Youth Corrections Act has given judges the option of using indeterminate sentencing.

The contrast between juvenile and adult court styles of disposition is substantial. What appears in a juvenile court as a high rate of informal disposition surfaces in the criminal court as a high rate of nonconviction. But the criminal court apparently gives more weight to the seriousness of the crime than does the juvenile court in dispositional decisions. In his study of the Manhattan Family Court, Paul Strassberg concluded that "roughly the same proportion [of violent and nonviolent delinquents] were placed or put on probation and a slightly greater proportion of violent offenders were released."[70] This study, like the preliminary data from Washington, D.C., in Tables II-1 and II-2, is based on a single set of observations of a single court at work. Yet it is plausible to suppose that the juvenile court, with its emphasis on the needs of children, would tend to make the seriousness of the offense less of a determinant of the sanction than it is in the criminal court, with its formal emphasis on the penal code.

What little is known of the treatment of the young offender in the adult criminal court suggests that sentencing policy takes youth and concomitant lack of an adult criminal record into account but is more offense-centered than sentencing policy in the juvenile court. Data on the treatment of the young in criminal courts are sorely needed. Age-specific studies of court processes are necessary because few formal legal distinctions are made within the criminal court between older and younger offenders. Certainly, the jurisdictional rubrics and dispositional rationales of adult and juvenile courts differ; but at present, we can only surmise the effects of those differences on the outcome of cases processed in the two institutions.

III/Mixed Motives:
On the Purposes of
Intervening in the
Lives of Young Offenders

Lawyers and social workers, for example, may well be reminded that the distinction between penal treatment and the administration of welfare services is one that has sometimes been far from clear, even in theory. This is especially likely to be true in a culture that tends to conceive of poverty, unemployment, and even physical handicaps as evidence of a lack of moral fiber in those who suffer such misfortunes. A striking illustration of this tendency is the movement during the sixteenth and seventeenth centuries that led to the establishment, in England and on the Continent, of the so-called houses of correction. Two historians of this movement state: "the essence of the house of correction was that it combined the principles of the poorhouse, workhouse, and the penal institution." Into these establishments were assembled with spectacular abandon, the widows, the orphans, the jobless and handicapped, beggars, prostitutes, and petty criminals—all for the greater glory of God, the reduction of the poor rates, and the enhancement of statistics of national production. Who will say that in present practice we have fully divorced ourselves from similar motivations.[1]

The contrast between what we say and what we do can be stark in a policy area generously endowed with both nostalgia and hard cases. Writing in 1909, Judge Julian Mack declared that the purpose of juvenile justice was

. . . not so much to punish as to reform, not to degrade but to uplift, not to crush but to develop, not to make him a criminal but a worthy citizen.[2]

Two years earlier, in the Cook County Juvenile Court's annual report, the

65

chief probation officer of the juvenile court had assumed a somewhat more pessimistic posture:

> All right-minded people are willing to have boys and girls have chances to do the right thing, but after they persistently throw chances away the same people would have a right to insist that these young people be really controlled, even if it takes the criminal court process to do it.[3]

Judge Mack was describing a therapeutic ideal. The chief probation officer was describing the troublesome cases that hampered the efficiency of his office, presenting a threat to the public, and challenged both his authority to supervise and his ability to cure. Any useful discussion of dispositional policy toward youth crime must sort out both sentimental generalizations about childhood and the punitive instincts that serious offenses and insubordination arouse.[4] The interplay between these modes of feeling dominates the debate on social policy toward young offenders.

The Young Offender as a Special Case

It is plausible to initiate such a discussion by asking: "Why should the state treat adolescents who have violated the law differently from other adolescents?" Or the discussion might begin with the question: "Why should the state treat adolescent offenders differently from other offenders?" In an important sense, each question answers the other and highlights the policy conflicts inherent in dealing with youth crime. Social policy toward youth calls for help and supervision. Social policy toward crime calls for suppression.

What distinguishes the young offender from other adolescents is the gravity of the specific offense that he has committed and its implications for the physical safety of the community, for the offender's life chances, and for a social order in which adults expect obedience from the young.[5] Yet a number of considerations that are part of our social policy toward youth also distinguish a young offender from an older individual who has committed the same crime. Immaturity is widely held to limit an individual's responsibility for his actions.[6] And because society assumes some responsibility for the education and socialization of the young, society may share some of the blame for a young offender's criminal acts, which manifest in part a failure to fulfill these obligations.[7]

At a different level, the statistical finding that individuals in their early teens are more crime-prone than other individuals suggests that youth crime is more often a symptom of a particular stage in personal development than the beginning of a criminal career. On this assumption, public policy should help young offenders, as far as is possible, to pass through this stage of development into law-abiding adulthood with their life chances intact.

Yet some aspects of social policy toward the young also argue for more intensive social control over youths, including young offenders, than over adults. This notion is the origin of the status offense—a legislative determination that certain forms of behavior in which adults may engage must be forbidden to the young. Emphasis on the special needs of the young for supervision permeates the provisions of the legal system for young persons in general.[8] Legislation dealing with the special needs of young offenders for supervision often asserts the value of early intervention in criminal careers and the notion that rehabilitation efforts are most appropriately directed at young offenders.[9]

Some of the above theories supporting special treatment for youthful offenders are debatable. Many are based on assumptions for which hard evidence is lacking. Yet they all play a role in shaping dispositional decisions and thus affect the lives of young offenders.[10]

The list of goals we pursue in dealing with young offenders is bewilderingly long. We wish to punish, and thus to achieve the incapacitative, deterrent, and retributive goals of punishment. We also wish to mitigate the harshness of punishment because of the offender's immaturity. To the extent that social policy toward youth crime is child-centered, we undertake to supervise the young in their continued development and emphasize the treatment and rehabilitation of young offenders. At the same time, we pursue policies of privacy, seeking to protect the young offender from the stigma normally associated with a criminal conviction.

The chaotic quality of much decisionmaking with regard to young offenders results, in large part, from conflicts between these objectives. For example, the goal of satisfying society's (or a particular victim's) need for retribution conflicts with the goal of protecting the youthful offender from stigma. The goal of incapacitating the offender (to prevent future crime) conflicts with that of protecting young offenders from loss of liberty. Punitive approaches intended to deter potential offenders conflict with benign approaches designed to rehabilitate the individual delinquent.

Less obvious, the different purposes of intervention also are a source of priority conflict in policymaking with regard to the young offenders. A system in which the only purpose of intervention was treatment would restrict its intervention to those cases most in need of treatment. A system solely concerned with the control of crime would reserve its largest interventions for its most serious repetitive offenders. A system dedicated exclusively to the supervision of young persons not conforming to the controls of parents and schools would restrict its intervention to the most disobedient. What of a system with all three motives?

Although disobedience, need for treatment, and persistent criminality may be simultaneously present in the behavior of some young offenders, the members of the youth population generally differ in their needs for supervision, treatment, and restraint from crime. In a system that emphasizes supervision, a fourteen-year-old female runaway and an alcohol-abusing teenager may be stronger candidates for secure confinement than a sixteen-year-old male burglar.[11] Children who sell drugs and children who buy drugs may represent similar supervisional problems from the standpoint of their welfare but sharply different cases in an intervention scheme based on crime control considerations.

Its mixed motives have made the juvenile court susceptible to two sorts of problems. The first is a form of common-sense algebra: the greater the number of purposes for intervention, the greater the number of interventions. If the juvenile court makes a serious effort to respond to almost all varieties of dysfunctional youthful behavior, large numbers of young people will find themselves involved with the juvenile court.[12] Criminal courts have been criticized recently for inefficiency because they fail to subject enough offenders to formal processing; juvenile courts, on the other hand, have been criticized for intervening in the lives of too many. It is quite possible that both criticisms are valid.

The second vulnerability of a multipurpose system is the opportunity it provides for false advertising—more precisely, for mislabeling the true motive for particular interventions. The literature of juvenile justice is replete with examples of punishment in the name of rehabilitation and the creation of "training schools" that operate on punitive or supervisory principles.[13] Not all of this mislabeling is deliberate. With so many announced purposes and so much ambivalence about treatment of young offenders, participants in the system may well misapprehend their own motives. Many parents can recall repeating phrases, such as "this is for your own good" and "this will hurt me more than it will hurt you," with a tone of near-conviction that made administering punishment easier. Yet a wide gap between announced and real motives is an evil in its own right and a significant obstacle to the principled formulation or reform of policy toward young offenders.

These problems are *not* unique to the juvenile court; they will exist in any institution that seeks to accommodate the conflicting purposes of social policy toward young offenders.

Mixing Motives—Policies Toward Young Offenders in Juvenile and Criminal Courts

Contrasting the institutional styles of juvenile and criminal courts in the processing of young offenders is a bit like contrasting the geography of an explored and an unexplored planet. At present, unfortunately, data on disposition of young offenders in criminal courts are scant. The emphasis on probation, the lack of correlation between crime rates and commitments to formal institutions, and the concentration of status offenders in detention and correctional institutions that characterize juvenile court processing suggest that juvenile court decisions are based in large part on supervision and treatment motivations.[14]

The criminal court is necessarily less concerned with supervision simply because it rarely deals with status offenders or children beyond control.[15] Fragmentary data suggest that the individualized justice of the criminal court for those young offenders who do fall within its jurisdiction is more strongly oriented toward crime control than is that of the juvenile court. A few states have special youth correctional acts that reflect some of the rehabilitative concerns typical of juvenile courts, stressing indeterminate sentences for young offenders.[16] But the overall response of the criminal court system to young offenders has not been studied in sufficient detail to allow confident generalizations.

Studies of differences in dispositional policy for a given age group processed in criminal court in some jurisdictions and in juvenile court in other jurisdictions would be particularly useful. Sixteen- and seventeen-year-old offenders are processed by the juvenile court in Philadelphia and by the criminal court in New York City. The differences between the two cities in formality of process, sanctioning policy, use and duration of probation, use and duration of detention, frequency and duration of incarceration, recidivism, and rates and patterns of youth crime could be explored in relatively straightforward comparative studies. Such studies have not been made, in part, perhaps, because many scholars consider the jurisdictional boundaries of the juvenile court as the end point for social policy toward young offenders.

The paucity of information about young offenders in criminal courts complicates the task of judging reform proposals that are intended to remedy the shortcomings of juvenile court processing of young offenders. Proposing reforms within this court or mechanisms of dealing with young offenders outside it inevitably involves guesswork because the known shortcomings of the juvenile court must be weighed against the unknown shortcomings of its alternatives.

IV / Some
Alternative Paths to Reform

A student of American culture might well be puzzled by the tone of most contemporary criticism of social policy toward young offenders. Crime is on the rise, and law-and-order rhetoric dominates public debate on criminal justice, but most reform proposals concerning juvenile justice favor lessening social control. Publicity about serious crimes committed by the young has produced several get-tough legislative proposals, but the recommendations of scholars and commissions are for "radical nonintervention,"[1] "locking them [juvenile offenders] out,"[2] and "the least restrictive alternative"[3] for disposing of youthful offenders.

Perhaps reformers and reform commissions are more softhearted than the general public. But the tenor of the rhetoric of reform in juvenile and criminal justice also may be related to a decline in emphasis on rehabilitation as a goal of sentencing. In the criminal justice system, the decline of rehabilitation has redirected attention to the other proclaimed motives of criminal law—retribution, deterrence, and incapacitation. In the juvenile court, loss of faith in rehabilitation has undermined the only announced purpose of the omnibus theory of delinquency, leaving the court without any formal rationale for intervention in the lives of its subjects.

General Consensus and Specific Disagreement

Apparent differences in contemporary reform proposals often shrink upon closer examination. For example, *Radical Nonintervention* is the title of a celebrated book by Edwin Schur. Much of Schur's analysis is indeed radical, but his prescription for dealing with serious youthful offenders is not:

> Individualized justice must necessarily give way to a return to the rule of law. This means that while fewer types of youthful behavior will be considered legal offenses, in cases of really serious misconduct such traditional

71

guidelines as specificity, uniformity and nonretroactivity ought to apply. Juvenile statutes should spell out very clearly just what kinds of behavior are legally prescribed, and should set explicit penalties for such violations (with perhaps a limited range of alternatives available to sentencing judges.)[4]

On this subject, Schur sounds as staid as a presidential commission. His proposal expresses a desire to return to principles of culpability from which young offenders have for the most part been exempted under the omnibus theory of delinquency.

Similarly, Jerome Miller, the architect of the first state program "to adopt and quickly implement a policy of closing down the traditional training schools,"[5] included as point seven in his deinstitutionalization policy "Acquisition of the new small intensive care security unit." The inclusion of this facility was felt necessary because the traditional training schools had served as symbols

> . . . of general deterrence, community protection and retribution. Even successful treatment on a community based program would not achieve this symbolic objective. . . . Most professionals agree that cases requiring security represent a small number, but they are the most troublesome for the local juvenile justice system to manage. There is, of course, wide disagreement about just which offenders merit this type of treatment.[6]

Schur and Miller are associated with extreme reformist positions in juvenile justice. Yet their ideas closely parallel the proposals in the mainstream juvenile justice standards project, which its chairman has labeled the "new pragmatism," and the earlier efforts of the President's Commission on Crime. In advocating "radical nonintervention" and "least restrictive alternative," respectively, Schur and Miller are not arguing that serious youth crime should be ignored but rejecting the omnibus theory of delinquency, which invokes the coercive power of the state in proportion to what a child needs rather than to what he has done.

The omnibus theory of delinquency and the broad reach of delinquency jurisdiction still have their defenders, but a consensus is forming among commissions and commentators in support of four basic juvenile justice reforms:

- narrowing the delinquency jurisdiction of the juvenile court

- reducing the number of youths placed under formal social control

- cutting back on state power to intervene coercively in the lives of young persons who have not violated the criminal law

- making the maximum amount of social control that can be imposed on young offenders proportional to the seriousness of their offenses.

Stated in such general terms, this reform agenda enjoys the support of the President's Commission on Crime, the Commission on Standards and Goals, the Juvenile Justice Standards volumes, and a majority of academic commentators.[7] But this consensus is qualified by two important facets of modern discussion of social policy toward youth crimes. First, most commentators are preoccupied by the omnibus theory of delinquency, and have devoted little time and thought to the "serious offender."[8] More extensive study of young people who have committed serious offenses and the treatment they receive in juvenile and criminal courts might lead to heated debate over what constitutes "seriousness" and what proportionality means in assessing the culpability of young offenders.[9] Second, to the extent that they have considered the details of policy toward young offenders, commentators differ substantially as to both the extent to which jurisdiction and power should be curtailed and the means they favor to achieve the four reforms on which they agree.

For example, almost all favor reducing state regulation of noncriminal misbehavior on the part of the young. But the measures proposed for this purpose range from total abandonment of coercive power over noncriminal behavior to simply keeping this noncriminal group out of secure institutions after adjudication.[10] Similarly, the consensus in favor of making the exercise of coercive state power more proportional to the seriousness of the youth offense coexists with a wide range of opinion on what constitutes proportional punishment. Thus, depending on which of many reform proposals is adopted, a sixteen-year-old convicted of murder may receive anything from a maximum of twenty-four months in secure custody to the death penalty.[11]

The different approaches to reform vary in both style and substance. For status offenses and undesirable but noncriminal behavior, some reformers, apparently including Schur,[12] would limit the state to supplying only voluntary social services. The Juvenile Justice Standards scheme would provide the state with some "crisis intervention" authority in the short term but would rely on the child's consent to accept treatment following "noncriminal misbehavior" and does not suggest any official response to those youngsters presently classified as status offenders because they abuse substances, such as alcohol or tobacco, that are forbidden to minors.[13] Other proposals to de-emphasize the role of the juvenile court in "status offense" involve the creation of entire new networks of "community-based" programs for status offenders, "predelinquents," and other children considered to be in need of state supervision.[14] The federal Juvenile Justice and Delinquency Prevention Act of 1974[15] seems to provide for some degree of coercive state power to channel status offenders into such community-based programs. Proposals to remove coercive state power probably would bring fewer adolescents under state supervision. Proposals involving the use of the juvenile court's coercive power as a backup to a new network of treatment would probably increase the number of agencies exercising social control over young persons and the number of young persons involved in the totality of the youth control system. Yet the proponents of both approaches maintain that their primary purpose is to reduce the use of the juvenile justice system to deal with status offenders.

Similarly, in dealing with the young offender, many proposals for proportionality in sentencing policy retain both the juvenile court and the status of delinquency. These proposals approach proportionality by defining different grades of delinquency and assigning different maximum sentences to these separate grades.[16] These proposals retain the existing vocabulary and legislative framework of the juvenile court as a mechanism for reform. At the other extreme, proposed Canadian legislation would abolish both the concept of delinquency and the title of juvenile court in favor of a "court for young offenders."[17] Substantial arguments can be made for both of these approaches. The case for renaming the institutions that deal with young offenders now within the jurisdiction of the juvenile court is, of course, that if we reject the omnibus theory of delinquency the child-centered court that was organized around that theory should be abolished. The case for retaining the old labels but reforming the consequences of labeling rests more on political than on jurisprudential considerations. The juvenile court is an existing, powerful, and resilient institution that currently achieves some protection for some young offenders. Working within present jurisdictional rubrics and terms would probably generate less political opposition than discarding the labels as well as the content of the omnibus theory of delinquency.

Some Perspectives on Reform Proposals

Although recent efforts to reform juvenile justice have been thoughtful and constructive, much of the recent literature on the subject is deficient in three important respects. First, many youth crime proposals come to different conclusions, not because their proponents have different ideological backgrounds but because they focus on different archetypical cases. Second, some proposals intended to achieve greater uniformity in the juvenile court might achieve that objective but create greater disparity between the adolescent in juvenile court and the adolescent in criminal court because they do not deal with the latter. Third, proposals for alternatives to the omnibus theory of delinquency fail to provide a principled basis for differentiation among the various forms of youth criminality.

Paradigm Cases: Different Theories for Different Problems.   Proposals for juvenile court reform differ in part because different commentators have had different typical cases in mind. Most runaways with whom the juvenile court deals, for example, are in early or middle adolescence.[18] Perhaps for that reason, the Juvenile Justice Standards volume on "noncriminal misbehavior" asserts that "the juvenile's acts of misbehavior, ungovernability, or unruliness which do not violate the criminal law should not constitute a ground for asserting juvenile court jurisdiction."[19] The Standards volume requires the consent of the child to his return to parent or guardian. Such policies may or may not make sense when applied to a fifteen-year-old child in conflict with his family who has run away from home. But as written, they appear to apply with equal force to seven-year-old children.[20] Such a curtailment of parental power over seven-year-olds is a sharp departure from common law and constitutional standards of parental control and appears to be quite a different issue from the same policy applied to children eight years older. Was this delegation of power to seven-year-olds intended? Or is it an example of an analysis that began with a single paradigm case and proceeded to the formulation of standards without regard to all the other instances of the problem?

The problem of stereotyping issues in terms of particular age groups is pervasive in juvenile justice and juvenile justice reform. For example, the merits of radical nonintervention would appear to depend heavily on the age of the child being discussed. Any balanced agenda of reform must be prepared to recognize the great differences among children in different developmental phases both before and within adolescence and to respond with something other than a single standard to the great variety of problems that different forms of deviance by the young represent.

A similar problem of stereotyping exists in much of the public debate over what to do with "the violent young offender." Public and legislative concern about violent crimes committed by young people tends to crystallize around well-publicized and unrepresentative episodes of violent crime committed by young offenders. On occasion, these well-publicized stereotypical cases become a basis for policy recommendations. Yet a case on the front page of *The New York Times* may mislead readers, causing them to form an image of "the violent offender" and apply it to the arrest and court processing statistics on "violent crime."[21] The four offenses that are generally aggregated and reported by the FBI as violent crime are homicide, rape, robbery, and aggravated assault. Homicide and rape are candidates for the front page, particularly when the offender is young and the victim is old, vulnerable, or well known.[22] Yet 90 percent of all youth arrests for violent crime are for robbery and aggravated assault.[23] Moreover, the 133,000 arrests made in 1975 for robbery and aggravated assault varied dramatically in seriousness and extent of offender involvement. Most of the victims of aggravated assaults by young offenders also are young, and the crime itself encompasses a range of acts from fistfights through shootings.[24] Most offenders under twenty who engage in robbery are unarmed rather than armed, and arrests for both robbery and assault often involve a large number of accessories as well as principal offenders.[25] To think of a single category of "the violent offender" under such circumstances is to be misled in a profoundly dangerous way.

The Problem of Systemic Impact.   A second pervasive problem in the literature on juvenile justice reform is a failure to recognize the broader implications of decisional principles applied to the juvenile court. For example, according to the waiver provisions of the Juvenile Justice Standard Act, a juvenile never before convicted of offenses involving violence cannot be waived out of the juvenile court, and even if he is currently charged with murder,[26] the maximum sentence he may receive is twenty-four months in a secure facility. Within the juvenile court, there may be much to recommend such an approach. From the broader perspective of a social policy toward youth crime, such a standard seems arbitrary. In a jurisdiction that defines the eighteenth birthday as the age limit for juvenile court processing, a seventeen-year-old willful killer will face a maximum penalty of twenty-four months' confinement; an eighteen-year-old may face the death penalty for the same offense. The requirement of a prior adjudication for a violent offense before any juvenile misconduct is waivable has two paradoxical effects: first, it may subject two juvenile killers to grossly different punishments if one has a prior record within the juvenile court and the other does not. If waiver to the criminal court depends on prior juvenile record, the killer who is waived to the criminal court because of his previous history of adjudication for a violent offense can rightly claim that it is his prior juvenile offense rather than the crime of which he is accused that has resulted in his unfavorable treatment.[27] Second, a tight waiver standard increases the importance of the arbitrary jurisdictional age boundary between juvenile and criminal courts.

The more we reform the juvenile system without regard for the treatment of young offenders in criminal court, the farther we stray from continuity and consistency in overall sentencing policy. The difficulty of fashioning standards for waiver is, in my judgment, a symptom of failure to approach reforming youth crime policy as an inter- rather than an intra-institutional problem. Certainly, immaturity may be considered to carry with it diminished responsibility, but reforming only one part of the dual system that deals with youthful offenders may create more disparity in treatment of essentially similar conduct than it alleviates.

Treating Different Cases Differently. The reform literature suggests that, unless one is prepared to swallow the omnibus theory of delinquency whole, it is not the age of the offender so much as his particular circumstances that should determine social policy toward his conduct. To consider the bank robber and the bicycle thief under the same jurisdictional rubric with the same dispositional alternatives is to endorse a theory of juvenile delinquency that is either obsolete or fading quickly. To proceed in any *other* manner toward reform is to consider the different types of youth deviance as representing different bases for the imposition of coercive state controls.

If runaway and robber are different social problems, and if the concept of proportionality in sanctions for youthful offenders is carried to the logical conclusion of different sanction alternatives, we must cease to consider children as a categorical grouping independent of the acts they commit. We must instead consider different classes of criminal offenses and offenders as special cases.

This relatively simple shift in focus has two consequences for the analysis of juvenile court processes. First, within the juvenile court, an emphasis on proportionality leads necessarily to a jurisprudence closer to that of criminal courts than of traditional juvenile justice jurisdiction. We move closer to making the punishment fit the crime and farther away from the treatment ideology and omnibus theory that have characterized juvenile delinquency jurisdiction in years gone by.

Second, the emphasis on the degree of seriousness or dangerousness of juvenile behavior also calls into question the appropriateness of the border between juvenile and criminal jurisdiction. The more closely the dispositional principles of the juvenile court resemble those of the criminal court, the more apparent become those differences in consequence that attach to juvenile as opposed to criminal court jurisdiction. Once the all-encompassing theory of delinquency is abandoned, the similarity between older juveniles and younger nonjuveniles also becomes more apparent; any disparity in the treatment of these two groups becomes, more clearly, an occasion for questioning the present dual system.

The Search for Principles

The conflicts inherent in sentencing young offenders do not disappear with the invocation of a magic word, such as "proportionality." Balancing the interests discussed in Chapter III remains a necessary part of setting punishments for young offenders.

All of the detailed commentaries on policy toward youth crime that invoke principles of proportionality also call for substantially shorter maximum periods of incarceration for convicted youthful offenders. For example, the Juvenile Justice Standards volume on sanctions sets forth a concept of proportional sentencing in which the maximum penalty available for a juvenile offender is totally determined by the maximum punishment provided by a particular state legislature for an adult who commits the same crime.[28] But the differences in the quantities of punishment available are substantial, as Table IV-1 shows.

Table IV-1 Maximum Penalty by Class of Offense

	Ages 18 and older	Ages 10–17
Class 1	Life or Death	2 Years
Class 2	20 Years	1 Year
Class 3	1 Year	6 Months
Class 4	Less than 1 Year	3 Months[a]

[a]Secure facility only if prior record.

Reprinted with permission from *Standards Relating to Juvenile Delinquency and Sanctions* [tentative draft]
Copyright © 1977 by Ballinger Publishing Company

Such a scheme is proportional only in the sense that the maximum criminal court penalty determines the maximum juvenile court sanction. But without considering the proportionality of sentences for adult offenders, the authors of the Standards volume arrived at arbitrarily varying ratios between adult and juvenile sentences. The maximum penalties for juvenile offenders are only fractions of those for adult offenders—one year instead of twenty for "class 2" offenses. A seventeen-year-old convicted of murder will serve far less time than is authorized for an eighteen-year-old convicted of a "class 2" offense. For an eighteen-year-old, the distinction between a "class 2" and "class 3" offense can mean a difference of nineteen years' imprisonment; for a seventeen-year-old, the difference in maximum penalties for the two offenses is six months.

Discontinuities of this kind would be troublesome under any system. When they occur in a system that espouses proportionality as its aim and uses adult sentences rather than theories of delinquency as the point of reference for juvenile sanctions, the contrasts are all the more noticeable and disturbing.

Where, then, does one look to find principles for constructing a unified approach to sentencing young offenders?

The criminal codes and case law in most states are silent on the sentencing of young offenders. They hide whatever special policies might exist behind the judicial and prosecutorial discretion in criminal sentencing. Those few jurisdictions that have special youth corrections acts are not promising models: these acts generally provide for indeterminate sentences and represent an extension of the same rehabilitative logic that generated the omnibus theory of delinquency.[29]

The general argument for proportionality in criminal sentences means either a return to the discretion that governs the criminal court or a search for new principles. It is a singular tribute to the unpopularity of the omnibus theory of delinquency that its critics are willing to fall back on the uncertainties of adult criminal sentences in their pursuit of reform.[30] In the current state of American criminal law, an appeal to proportionality is not a solution to the issue of policy for young offenders; it is a method of starting from scratch.

As a starting point, reform requires principles to explain legal response to youth crime. The two most plausible justifications for separate treatment of adolescent offenders are the social value of giving young offenders the chance to mature and the theory that offenses committed by adolescents are less blameworthy than those committed by adults because the offender is not fully mature. Both of these principles justify lenient treatment of young offenders, but they differ in a number of other respects.

Room to Reform. One function of social policy toward young offenders is to provide the opportunity for them to outgrow a developmental stage that is peculiarly vulnerable to pressures toward criminality. The intense concentration of some property offenses among adolescents suggests that most people who commit such offenses during adolescence cease to commit them upon attaining adulthood. One purpose of mitigating the harshness of punishment for young offenders is to enhance the opportunity to survive adolescence without a major sacrifice in life chances. In providing the opportunity, a community deliberately takes risks with the auto thief, just as it takes risks with the young driver.

Advocating "room to reform" for young offenders is not the equivalent of saying that criminal acts committed by the young should go unpunished. Punishment may be an appropriate response to youth crime. But a policy that facilitates growth is one that avoids permanent stigma, the isolation of young offenders from community settings, or any other form of exile from the larger society in which they are expected to grow.

A general policy of giving young offenders the opportunity to learn from and survive adolescent misdeeds represents an intelligent social policy option as a value decision independent of whatever empirical data we have that suggests it is "cost effective"; values may dictate policies designed to achieve these ends, even if a substantial minority of the young do not outgrow patterns of law violation.[31]

Perhaps American adolescents should not be age-segregated and dependent.[32] But the social meaning of adolescence was not invented by adolescents. Our culture views the adolescen⁺ years as a transition—frequently a troublesome transition—to adulthood. Social policy toward the young offender should be designed, as much as is practical, not to diminish the individual's chances to make that transition successfully.

The concept of "room to reform" differs from the concept of rehabilitation, which relies on coercive state power to socialize and mature young offenders. The advocates of rehabilitation envisioned a curing process in which treatment produced results in a relatively passive subject. Underlying the concept of providing room to reform are the notions that reform is a process in which time, the offenders' efforts, and the resources in the community at large play their parts; the use of coercive state power may sometimes unduly disrupt this process. This is not to say that the state plays or should play a neutral role in individual growth. Better educational and social services and greater social and economic opportunities for the young probably facilitate growth in the lives of all young people, particularly those most at risk during adolescence. But these aspects of social policy toward youth are not crime-specific, nor do they amount to the compulsory moral rearmament favored by the most extreme advocates of rehabilitation.

Diminished Responsibility. Another rationale for separate treatment of young offenders is diminished responsibility on account of immaturity. If proportionality were the sole consideration in sentencing, many young offenders would receive harsher punitive treatment than that meted out to most adult offenders. Sound sentencing policy also takes into account the forces that impinge on adolescent life, including the adolescent's shaky judgment and incapacity to resist peer pressure. The concept of diminished responsibility on account of immaturity means that young offenders should be treated more leniently than adult offenders not because their acts are less dangerous but because they are less capable of controlling impulses, resisting peers, or thinking in the long-range terms that characterize mature decisionmaking. The implications of diminished responsibility are paradoxical: we punish those who are greater risks to the community more leniently precisely because of the conditions that make them greater risks.

Precedents for this type of policy appear in the criminal law of insanity, intoxication, and mental instability. Some of these conditions provide a complete defense against criminal liability.[33] Adolescence clearly should not be in this category, unless one is prepared to argue that the condition of adolescence in American society totally deprives the affected individual of the capacity to know right from wrong or to resist any impulse. More instructive are the mitigations of punishment available for the mentally disturbed, who are held partially accountable for their acts. Their criminal behavior is considered blameworthy but *less* so than that of a mentally normal individual.[34] Adolescents have had some experience in making moral decisions but not so much experience as adults and far fewer opportunities than adults have had for exercising responsibility in making decisions.

A diminished responsibility policy, given the reasoning behind it, should operate on a sliding scale. Just as the adolescent is held less morally responsible than the adult, a fourteen-year-old is presumptively entitled to a greater degree of mitigation of blameworthiness than an eighteen-year-old. Similarly, chronological age cannot be the sole basis for determinations of maturity; the different capacities and life circumstances of two sixteen-year-olds may call for different gradations of the criminal sanction.

In theory, the notion of diminished responsibility due to immaturity applies to the full range of criminal offenses. Yet considerations of diminished responsibility have more pronounced effects on sentencing for the very serious offenses that normally mandate the most awesome of criminal punishments than on sentencing for more trivial offenses. The greater the otherwise available sanction, the greater the practical weight of diminished responsibility as a mitigation of that sanction. Moreover, the more bizarre the criminal behavior, the more likely are the circumstances of the offender to suggest diminished responsibility. Thus, diminished responsibility is one of the more dramatic doctrinal examples in the criminal law of the conflict between utilitarian and retributive theories of justice for young offenders. It is the retributive rather than the utilitarian branch of the justification for criminal punishments that provides a basis for diminished responsibility as a major force in determining punishments for young offenders.

As reform efforts move to a system of proportional punishments, the principles of diminished responsibility and of giving opportunity for growth emerge as coherent motives for differential leniency in the sentencing of young offenders. These are the explicit theories on which many of the following policy suggestions are based. These theories do not correspond to any current jurisdictional borders between juvenile and criminal courts. Rather, they extend across the ill-defined frontiers of adolescence and challenge reform efforts to deal with a broader spectrum of young offenders.

V / Policy Options
for Young Offenders

A range of policy options is available for different types of youth crimes and for noncriminal misbehavior now within the jurisdiction of the juvenile court. In the following discussion of sentencing policies in juvenile and criminal courts, I assume a system in which delinquency jurisdiction (or its equivalent) covers acts committed before an offender's eighteenth birthday. The analysis of noncriminal misbehavior includes only those acts currently within the delinquency or "persons in need of supervision" jurisdiction of the juvenile court.[1]

Noncriminal Misbehavior and Status Offenses—
Acts against Parental and State Authority

A set of special obligations accompanies the special protections of American childhood. Children must go to school and obey their parents or other custodial adults. Acceptance of these obligations is not universal. State power to intervene coercively in the lives of disobedient, truant, and runaway children is older than the juvenile court and an important contemporary part of the court's jurisdiction. As Professor Gough has written:

> Jurisdiction over noncriminal misbehavior is both widespread and widely invoked. Every juvenile court law has some ground or grounds extending the court's power of intervention to cases involving antisocial but noncriminal behavior. Such cases probably comprise—though firm figures are not available—no less than one-third and perhaps close to one-half of the work load of America's juvenile courts.[2]

Either for their own protection or for that of the community, young people in the United States also are typically denied privileges available to adults. Thus, young persons under specified statutory ages are prohibited

83

from smoking, driving, drinking, possessing firearms, and staying on the streets past "curfew." The prohibitions on smoking and drinking are probably more closely associated with protecting the young person than with protecting the community. The prohibitions on driving, possession of firearms, and violating the curfew may have more to do with community protection.[3] When young people violate these prohibitions, they subject themselves to legal liability for acts that would not be criminal if committed by adults. In much of the literature on juvenile justice, noncriminal misbehavior and conduct that is criminal solely because of the offender's youth are aggregated and termed "status offenses." In this chapter, the term "status offense" applies only to the latter type of act because the two types of behavior are significantly different. The only offense that does not clearly fall into one category or the other is truancy.[4]

Under the omnibus theory of delinquency, the truant, the runaway, the curfew violator, and the drinker are delinquents;[5] under reform statutes, runaways and truants are subdelinquent "persons in need of supervision."[6] Modern reform literature, particularly proposals focused on noncriminal misbehavior, argues that the pejorative labeling of disobedient children as protocriminal and the shipment of such children to secure custodial facilities are inappropriate.[7] There the consensus ends.

Most reform proposals, even those designed to de-institutionalize children accused of noncriminal misbehavior, call for using the jurisdiction of the juvenile court (or some variant of the family court) as a backup to voluntary services and nonsecure placements assigned to help the juvenile in conflict with his family. A separate line of analysis, originating in the President's Crime Commission, questions the very exercise of juvenile court jurisdiction over noncriminal misbehavior.[8] Many academic commentators have suggested that the disobedient child is an inappropriate object for juvenile court intervention, and the Juvenile Justice Standards suggest that, except for temporary crisis intervention power, state law should give the disobedient child's wishes precedence over those of his parents and the state.[9]

If the emphasis of juvenile court jurisprudence is to shift toward retribution and away from supervision, parent-child conflicts seem inappropriate for juvenile court processing. Whatever one may say about the proper power relationship between parent and child,[10] a child who disobeys his or her parents obviously should not incur criminal sanctions. But although the use of coercive state power to back up parental authority may be difficult to distinguish from punishment, it is not inherently incorrect. Noncriminal misbehavior involves a variety of problems: a fifteen-year-old runaway boy or girl in conflict with parents, a pregnancy in early teenage years, and sexual acting out (for boys as well as girls) that runs the high risks of pregnancy or criminal behavior. All of these cases may be inappropriate for punishment but not necessarily inappropriate for coercive state intervention. Whether the state should back up parental authority (and substitute for that authority where it does not exist) or adopt a hands-off policy is not best addressed as an issue of abstract principle. Rather, it should be an empirically based choice—between the dangers of overintervention and those of underintervention—of the less harmful alternative. The category of noncriminal misbehavior covers a variety of cases, and the degree of state power that should be brought to bear in a particular situation may be difficult to determine. Probably, social policy should start with a presumption of nonintervention but should make that presumption susceptible to disproof when, because of a youth's incapacity for mature decisionmaking,[11] a hands-off policy is inappropriate. In the parent-child setting, the law must be flexible enough to recognize the difference between seven- and seventeen-year-olds in making decisions about whether the parents' wishes or the child's should prevail. When the state is being asked to function in the absence of parental control, social policy should probably be different, depending on whether the child is simply disobedient or, for example, an incipient alcoholic.[12] State power in these cases need not be centered in the juvenile court and should not involve the label of delinquency.

If the state cuts back on delinquency jurisdiction for noncriminal misbehavior, it also should make a commitment to the provision of services for the child at war with the values or custody of his family. Warm, receptive nonsecure facilities providing quasi-parental care would make juvenile court jurisdiction less necessary and state intervention less onerous. But designing and operating such facilities are difficult given the well-documented scarcity of adequate social services.[13] Persistently disobedient children are among the most difficult cases encountered by the courts, social agencies, and institutions that handle them. This is an area where there are no totally right answers.

Complete abandonment of juvenile court jurisdiction over such cases would be a radical departure from American family law unless some court retained the power to intervene to reinforce parental power or to substitute for the power of absent parents in much the same way that the juvenile court exercises its neglect and dependency jurisdiction.[14] Clearly, the juvenile court must proceed with caution in dealing with parent-child conflicts. Yet some basis for arbitrating between the claims of the parent and those of the child in light of the state's conception of the child's best interest will be necessary within the context of the court system for some time to come.

The status offender, as defined here, presents different problems. The prohibitions that are designed to protect the immature from harming themselves—such as those on drinking, smoking, and perhaps truancy—seem at first glance inappropriate candidates for a punishment policy. Punishing a child for using harmful substances seems to place him in double jeopardy—

from both the harmful act and its punishment in the name of social protection. Yet some measure of punishment for violation of social prohibitions that are age-related is not intrinsically inappropriate. The extent of punishment for these offenders is the key issue. In any scheme of proportional punishments, those status offenders who risk only harm to themselves must be considered low on the list of subjects for coercive social control.[15] But again, it is pragmatism rather than principle that should determine the measure of social control to be directed against this variety of status offender.

Such laws as curfews and prohibitions of underage youth driving or acquiring firearms are meant to protect both the community at large and the young themselves. Punishment for violations of those prohibitions is an appropriate option for the juvenile court. In this area (and the closely related area of drug-law enforcement[16]), the volume of youth criminality is a natural constraint on sanctioning policy.[17] The sheer size of the status offender population, coupled with the low individual risk associated with any particular status offense, makes informal dispositions and only extremely limited use of coercive power the most practical mechanisms available to the juvenile court. Both the numbers and the relative triviality of status offenses argue for low and nonincarcerative sanction policies.

Neither the omnibus theory of delinquency (which underlies juvenile court jurisdiction over "children in need of supervision") nor the almost total hands-off policy of the tentative Juvenile Justice Standards volumes[18] fits all cases comfortably. The omnibus theory casts its net too widely into the pool of youth misconduct. But a policy of "benign neglect," abandoning all bases for coercive state intervention, seems irresponsible. Public policy should seek a workable middle ground. But those who would use the juvenile court to protect the rebellious young must bear in mind that, often, coercive state power may simply be too blunt an instrument for the purpose.

Sentencing Policy Toward Young Property Offenders

Vandalism, auto theft, larceny, and burglary are disproportionately activities of the young. All are crimes against property, but vandalism and burglary, unlike auto theft and larceny, also contain elements of intimidation that generate fear in victims. None of these offenses carries a significant risk of victim death or serious bodily injury.[19]

Dispositional policy toward this class of property offender is critical to both juvenile and criminal courts because these offenses comprise a majority of all cases that come before the court, juvenile or criminal, that deals with young offenders. Although in many of these cases, some punishment is warranted, the current system appears muscle-bound: it does either too much—incarcerating juvenile offenders adjudicated for such offenses—

or too little—assigning unconditional discharges or almost meaningless probation as punishment for serious offenses.

In major urban areas, the majority of offenders charged with such crimes are handled informally and thus are unaffected by formal sanctions policy. In informal disposition, the juvenile exchanges due process for leniency. The sacrifice of due process probably is necessary, given the large volume of adolescent property crimes. But these conditions frustrate attempts to read principle into the disposition of offenders.

The rate of property offenses committed by the young is likely to remain high. This assumption is based, in part, on skepticism about the effects of the sanctions delivered by the legal system on youth criminality. But policies of minimal intervention may be justified even if society pays a measurable price in increased property criminality. A social policy of protecting the young may have other benefits that justify lesser punishment for the vandal, shoplifter, and juvenile burglar even if more repressive measures would produce lower rates of these offenses. Moreover, punishment is not the only available mode of social defense against these forms of adolescent criminality. For example, it may be better to prevent auto theft and burglary with steering-wheel locks and window locks than to sentence juvenile car thieves and burglars to long periods of incarceration.

Four specific proposals that could reshape sanctioning policy toward property offenders in the juvenile court are:

- the creation of guidelines to lend principle to the exercise of low visibility discretion in the informal disposition of property offenders

- a presumption against secure custodial disposition for juvenile property offenders

- experimentation with intermediate, openly punitive sanctions for juvenile property offenders

- the creation of relatively low maximum durations of secure confinement for juveniles convicted of property offenses.

Guidelines for Police and Intake Decisionmaking.   Much of the decisionmaking about sanctioning policy for property offenders involves the discretion of police to arrest or to station-adjust (i.e., to dispose of charges without arrest). It also involves the discretion of intake workers in juvenile courts to choose between formal and informal processing for the juvenile accused of a property crime; thus, a necessary first step in a reasoned policy toward juvenile property offenders is the structuring of guidelines so that decisions of whether or not to arrest and whether or not to process a juvenile formally are phrased in comprehensible policy terms.

Guidelines for intake discretion would include such obvious factors as the seriousness of the offense (e.g., property loss and the risk of collateral harm), the extent to which the particular adolescent was a dominant as opposed to a passive accomplice in the offense, the prior police record of the offender, and a ban (difficult to enforce) on the use of preadjudication detention for the purpose of punishment as an alternative to formal processing.

It is much harder to devise guidelines than to engage in the more popular exercise of insisting that guidelines are necessary. It is possible to provide police and intake workers with a rough measure of the seriousness of a particular property offense. It is probably impossible to give police and intake workers precise guidelines as to when the seriousness of the property crime committed by one youth or the importance of the role played in a multiple-offender crime by another justifies subjecting him to formal processing. Where information systems are coordinated so that information about an individual's criminal record is available to police and intake workers, guidelines could include a presumption against formal processing for juveniles charged with property offenses short of burglary, who have never before been *arrested* for serious offenses, and leave substantial discretion for informal processing of juvenile offenders arrested for burglary.

The intake worker's discretion to process formally or informally is essentially a punishment decision. Hence, it may be argued that data on prior arrests that did not result in a finding of guilt should not be used to govern later discretion about whether to pass a juvenile on toward formal processing. However, the alternative to using prior unproven charges as a basis for passing a juvenile into formal processing is allowing an often-arrested juvenile to remain a perpetual first offender. Both options carry substantial costs. However, since the decision to process an accused formally is not an adjudication of the case on the merits, the use of prior police contacts can be justified.

Guidelines would help to reduce discrepancies but could not eliminate them, both because it is impossible to determine and to weight accurately all of the factors that should lead to diversion or passing on in the system and because, when the power to make decisions is decentralized and not highly visible, precise guidelines are difficult to enforce. Yet rationalizing punishment policy toward juvenile property crime must begin at the beginning.

Restricting Secure Confinement for Property Offenders.   The widely invoked "least restrictive alternative" in sentencing policy for juvenile offenders has never been defined in terms that command consensus. My own view is that the definition should include a presumption against secure confinement for juveniles adjudicated for commission of property offenses. The circumstances that could rebut that presumption would include either extraordinarily serious current charges or previous adjudications involving serious property crime or worse.

Obviously, this dispositional policy precludes the incarceration of first offenders in the absence of extraordinary circumstances. In fact, in conjunction with my recommendation regarding intake discretion, this policy would exclude most first and *second* offenders from eligibility for secure, postadjudication custodial confinement. The presumption is thus a rough "three strikes and you may be out" formula. To the extent that prospective young offenders view alternatives to incarceration as a "free ride," a relatively inflexible policy of using these alternatives to incarceration for first convictions may be less effective as a deterrent than the unspecified risk of incurring sanctions that present statutes provide.

Also, like all presumptive rather than proscriptive policies, this one leaves different judges free to treat similar cases in different ways. (In practice, trial judges rather than the appellate bench largely determine the extent to which presumptions govern case flow and reduce disparity.) Any approach that has the virtue of permitting judges to tailor sentences for unusual cases also retains the risk of sentencing disparity in the system as a whole.

A presumption against secure confinement for first adjudicated property offenders differs more in theory than in practice from present dispositional policy. In theory, a policy of early intervention strategy for the purpose of rehabilitation is incompatible with policy of avoiding custodial confinement until a relatively late point in a young offender's career. In practice, in 1975 only 3.8 percent of all juveniles arrested in Cook County for the offense of burglary were committed to the Department of Corrections.[20] The proposed policy would alter practice only to the extent that it reduced the use of punitive detention.[21]

Intermediate Sanctions for Juvenile Property Offenses. If punitive detention is to be discarded and secure custody reserved for persistent recidivists, the legal system must still respond appropriately in the commission of nonchronic but (in varying degrees) serious crimes. The state might express disapproval of such acts through a series of intermediate, frankly punitive sanctions that intrude less profoundly on the life of the young offender than secure confinement but extend beyond the tokenism of probation in most of the juvenile courts in the country. Some examples of intermediate penal sanctions are the forced work euphemistically called the "community service order" in those jurisdictions that have used it,[22] restitution to victims (which typically involves coerced participation in income-producing activities),[23] and loss of privileges such as driving. Such other alternatives to incarceration as coercive referrals to group psychotherapy, counseling, or youth "diversion" programs are not, strictly speaking, penal measures, even though the young offender involved may regard coercion to treatment as punitive. Other possible intermediate sanctions are less promising in the juvenile courts. For example, the use of substantial fines in juvenile court would generally shift the burden from the juvenile to his parents and, in many cases, might impose undeserved hardships on them.

Any experiment with intermediate sanctioning policy will encounter the problem of what to do with the young offender if he fails to meet the conditions of an intermediate sanction order, such as a restitution or community service order. Resort to secure confinement as a kind of punishment for contempt of court in such settings is expensive and difficult to justify.[24] The use of fines as an alternative to secure confinement is even less satisfactory because it gives the willingness or ability of parents to pay fines or make restitution too large a role in the choice of custodial or non-custodial treatment for offenders.[25]

Any experiment with intermediate sanctioning also must confront the trade-off between due process and leniency inherent in the juvenile and criminal courts. Ideally, the assignment of an intermediate sanction would follow formal adjudication of the offender's guilt in the juvenile court. But the pressure of numbers and the reliance on informality in the present system suggest that, in practice, programs of restitution and community service also are likely to be used in the bargaining over formal or informal disposition. Presumptions against secure custody and punitive detention may serve, to some extent, to prevent such an undesirable relocation of sentencing power by creating a class of offender with little to lose in formal processing. However, any proposal to reduce the juvenile court's discretionary power to induce minors to waive their rights to expensive, formal, and time-consuming adjudication in exchange for less coercive treatment is likely to encounter substantial political opposition.

Maximum Sentences for Juvenile Property Offenders.   On grounds of both diminished responsibility and deterrence, an integrated system of sanctioning policies toward young property offenders should probably provide relatively low maximum sentences for offenses that do not involve a substantial risk of bodily harm. This policy can be applied both in systems where correctional authorities rather than judges are responsible for determining time served and in systems where judges and correctional authorities share the power to determine time served.[26] The principle is incompatible with consecutive sentencing for multiple property offenses, which lengthens time served and thus blurs the distinction between violent and nonviolent offenses.[27] In making individual dispositional decisions, both judges and juvenile correctional authorities might take particular offenders' prior records into consideration, treating a prior record of property offenses as a necessary but not sufficient condition for a secure custodial sentence.

Some Alternative Approaches.   Implicit in this scheme is a rejection of both the discretion embodied in the omnibus theory of delinquency and the artificial precision of "presumptive sentences" of incarceration for property offenses. An alternative sentencing approach available to the juvenile court is the use of discretion without reference to the omnibus theory of delinquency. The only possible justification for giving a court the power to select any sentence (even within limits) for any offender within its jurisdiction is the motive of rehabilitation.

One alternative to discretion is a system in which each property crime carries a "presumptive" penalty to be imposed in the absence of aggravating or mitigating circumstances. The aims of this approach are to minimize sentence disparity and to assure that offenses are punished.[28] But a presumptive penalty approach is not well suited to custodial sentencing for juvenile property offenders. The high volume of arrests, the frequency of multiple-offender arrests, and de facto social tolerance of youth property crime have produced an extremely low rate of incarceration for property offenders in the juvenile court, particularly in m.jor urban areas. Any presumptive sentencing scheme that did not give heavy weight to prior records of adjudication would produce sentences radically different from those currently imposed on young offenders by juvenile courts. Any presumptive sentencing scheme that did give heavy weight to prior records of adjudication within the juvenile court in choosing between custodial and noncustodial sentences for property offenses would in fact be basing its decisions on the discretion formerly available to juvenile courts to select formal or informal processing for young offenders.[29]

Marvin E. Wolfgang of the University of Pennsylvania has proposed a system that would use total social harm inflicted by an offender, measured in scaled "points,"[30] as a basis for fixing punishment in juvenile court. The system is ingenious but is subject to manipulation both by police and intake workers in evaluating an offender's prior criminal record and by police alone in their discretion to use multiple charges as a basis for pushing an offender over the point threshold for coercive intervention. The "point" proposal differs from the use of prior records of adjudication because it gives the police the additional power to charge an offender with eight counts of burglary or larceny rather than one and thus makes persons who have no prior criminal records eligible for sentences of secure confinement.[31]

A number of commentators concerned with undue leniency in sentencing advocate schemes in which a discretionary sentencing or correctional authority determines the maximum sanction for a given offense but the minimum penalty is determined by the legislature. This mandatory minimum sanctions strategy has been most often proposed for use in the criminal courts, but some have urged mandatory minimum sanctions in the juvenile court as well. New York has recently passed a "designated felony" provision that applies to persons convicted of certain violent offenses in the juvenile court.[32]

The purpose of mandatory minimum sanctions for juvenile property crime is crime reduction. The extent of crime reduction that this expansion of social control might produce is the subject of heated debate, and reliable data that might help in resolving that debate are scarce.

The disadvantages of mandatory minimum sanctions, particularly those involving secure confinement for property offenders, are manifold. Given the huge volume of arrests, a formal mandatory minimum policy would widen the disparity in punishment between offenders adjusted informally (no minimum sentence) and offenders who are formally processed and subjected to the minimum sanction on conviction. Mandatory minimum custodial sanctions for property offenses also would cause a proliferation of plea negotiations and judicial findings motivated by the desire to avoid the mandatory sanction.

The adoption and use of mandatory minimum custodial sanctions would bring about a revolution in dispositional policy toward property crime by the young. At present, a juvenile arrested for burglary in Chicago faces a 4 percent chance of commitment to a state training school. The rates of institutionalization for lesser property crimes, such as auto theft, are even lower.[33]

A mandatory minimum approach employing sanctions other than secure confinement might be appropriate for some types of property crime. But the only alternative to incarceration that is now widely used in the juvenile courts is probationary supervision in the community. Although it is intellectually respectable to argue that conviction on a criminal burglary charge "deserves" at least probationary supervision, the widespread use of this sanction might overtax the probationary resources of many systems, and is unlikely to achieve the punitive and crime control goals that typically underlie the call for mandatory minimum sanctions.

Young Property Offenders in Criminal Court.   If there is merit to the argument that social policy toward the young offender should be coordinated across the boundary of juvenile and criminal courts, it is necessary to consider what criminal court sentencing policies would be appropriate for young offenders beyond the jurisdictional boundaries of the juvenile court. To be consistent with the policies proposed for the juvenile court, criminal court sentencing policies for property crimes would have to include a preference for the diversion of young first offenders and a presumption against incarceration for first offenders of all ages in the adult court. (This presumption, in practice, would primarily affect those offenders between sixteen or eighteen and twenty-one years of age.) A corollary to the low maximum sentence of incarceration for property offenders in juvenile court would be an explicit policy of low maximum sentences for younger property offenders in criminal court, although the criminal court maximum would be higher than the juvenile court maximum.

This type of criminal court policy has two practical consequences worthy of note. First, what scant information we have on the careers of young offenders in criminal courts suggests that such proposals amount to an endorsement of the status quo. The pattern of criminal court sentencing of young offenders implies that theories of diminished responsibility play a role in the sentencing decision. The adoption of a formal set of youth-centered principles would attach some theory to established practice.

Second, to the extent that juvenile and criminal court systems do not share information but do follow this type of sentencing policy, a young property offender could, theoretically, be apprehended a total of four times—twice in the juvenile system and twice thereafter—before he encounters the serious risk of incarceration. This price may be worth paying, but the combined effects of the information gap and the jurisdictional age boundary between the two court systems on the sentences received by young offenders are striking. Specifically, in a system with a low maximum juvenile court age, such as the sixteenth birthday, sixteen-year-olds may be treated more leniently in the criminal court, if it does not have access to their juvenile records at the critical early stages of case processing, than they would be in the juvenile court. The repetitive offender soon loses this benefit and, after two or three arrests in the criminal court system, is likely to be treated more severely than he would be, at the same age and with the same history, in a jurisdiction with a higher juvenile court age boundary.

There is no completely satisfactory solution to the problem of how and when information should be supplied by the juvenile justice system to the criminal justice system; values of privacy and protection must be balanced off against the anomalies that are produced when lack of prior record data influences criminal court policies. In their efforts to eliminate such anomalies from sentencing, policymakers also must accommodate these values.

Some Alternative Approaches.   In most jurisdictions, once an offender has aged out or has been waived out of the juvenile court, his youth has no formal relevance to the criminal sentence he may incur. In Connecticut, the sixteen- and twenty-six-year-old robber are, theoretically, equal in the eyes of the law. The discretion available to sentencing judges generally allows them to consider youth in mitigation of criminal sentences, but few states give explicit direction on this matter.[34] The purpose of this policy is to allow judges to tailor justice to each unique case that comes before them. The disadvantage of this approach is that it gives individual judges rather than the legislature the responsibility for setting social policy toward young offenders, and it probably leads to wide variation in the degree to which youth is considered as a mitigating circumstance. Under current conditions, the border between juvenile and adult court jurisdiction straddles three critical years of adolescent life, at varying points during which, depending on his geographical location, a young offender may experience "instant adulthood." If youth is to be a mitigating factor, total reliance on prosecutorial and judicial discretion to implement social policy toward young offenders in the absence of explicit policy seems inappropriate.

A few jurisdictions have adopted optional "young offender" acts that provide separate sentencing policy and correctional facilities for young offenders who are found eligible for such treatment. In most of these states, the judge retains the power to decide whether a young offender should be sentenced under the special provisions of these acts or as an adult. In New York, a judge may classify a sixteen-year-old armed robber as either a young offender subject to a maximum sentence of four years or an adult subject to a maximum sentence of twenty-five years.[35] Again, the argument in favor of such discretion is flexibility; the idea behind the act is to enable judges to treat the majority of young offenders leniently without denying them the use of harsher treatment for truly hardened criminals. But some commentators feel that only crimes that involve threats to human life can possibly call for the total sacrifice of an offender's life chances. The key issue in the decision to make special treatment of the young property offender in criminal courts optional or mandatory is whether or not property crime by adolescent offenders is considered potentially serious enough to call for longer terms of imprisonment than the maximums provided by young offender legislation.

In the minority of jurisdictions that have passed special young offender legislation, the maximum sanction available for the adolescent who is classified as a young offender is smaller than that available for the older offender for very serious crimes, but the "young offender" sentence is indeterminate in all cases.[36] A parole or correctional authority has discretion to judge the offender's progress in treatment and to predict the degree of risk that the community will run if he is released. As parole based on this sort of prediction passes out of style in both the juvenile and criminal justice systems, indeterminate sentences for the purpose of rehabilitation seem increasingly incongruous in young offender legislation.[37] Our capacity to rehabilitate offenders in prison settings seems minimal.[38] Our capacity to determine whether or not a former offender will abstain from criminal activity if released from prison is too insubstantial to provide the underlying rationale for criminal sentencing.[39]

It might be argued that once an offender has aged out of the juvenile justice system his age should not influence the decision as to his criminal sentence. Rejecting the importance of the rationales put forward earlier for special treatment of the young in the criminal court, a proponent of this position would argue that it is illogical to punish a twenty-eight-year-old first offender more harshly than an eighteen-year-old first offender simply for having waited ten years to commit (or be apprehended for) a crime. However, special policies of leniency toward the young do not necessarily preclude leniencies toward older offenders in special cases on other grounds. In the criminal courts of major metropolitan areas, twenty-eight-year-old first offenders who have committed property crimes are special cases. The mitigating factors in such cases are, however, different from those in cases involving adolescents. The sixteen-year-old may receive probation because he is immature and vulnerable to the pressures of adolescence, or because the benefits of allowing him an opportunity to mature without stigma outweigh the risk that he will use his freedom to engage in further criminal activity. The twenty-eight-year-old first offender will receive probation because he represents less of a risk to the community or because he has a long history of stable, law-abiding behavior. Sentencing and parole guidelines currently tend to give favorable treatment to persons with stable employment histories and marital situations, statuses more commonly found among adults than among adolescents.[40]

The ultimate argument against treating age as critically important in the juvenile court and irrelevant in the criminal court is that it has produced a mad pattern of cross-jurisdictional sentencing disparities. Any policy that does not deal with youth as a mitigating factor in the criminal court must be based on a considered judgment with these problems of disparity and arbitrariness can never be satisfactorily solved.

"Fixed price" or "presumptive" sentencing policies are widely advocated today as alternatives to the present heavily discretionary structure of sentencing power.[41] Any system of fixed price or presumptive sentencing that does not take youth into account can only magnify the differences between the disposition of the juvenile offender and the young offender in criminal court and create a jurisprudence of youth crime that operates with two mutually exclusive sentencing policies.

Violence, Proportionality, and the Young Offender

Acts of violence committed by the young are the worst cases of the conflict between protecting the young offender and protecting society and the hardest cases for which to fashion appropriate dispositional policies in juvenile and criminal courts. Violent crimes, unlike most property crimes, cannot be prevented by self-defense measures that carry tolerable costs: locking doors to prevent burglary makes sense; abandoning the streets to avoid physical danger seriously infringes on the rights of individuals. Many violent offenses involve victim death or serious injury. A free society cannot indefinitely bear the costs of high rates of violent criminality.

Yet what the police and the media term "violent crime" varies in seriousness from fistfights to homicide, and sentencing policy toward violent crimes committed by the young requires distinguishing among offenses of violence as well as between violent and nonviolent offenses. Ninety percent of all police arrests of the young for offenses of violence involve robbery and aggravated assault. In both of these categories, the difference between two individual crimes may be as great as the difference between violent and nonviolent crime.[42] Aggravated assault encompasses fistfights that carry no risk of death, as well as shootings that are separated from homicide only because of modern medicine and fortuity. Robbery, the taking of property by the use or threat of force, inevitably exposes the victim to the risk of injury, but the victim's death risk in an unarmed robbery is one-tenth that of the victim of an armed robbery,[43] and the victim's death risk in an armed robbery is a fraction of that generated by an aggravated assault involving firearms.[44] Intentional homicide and rape are, obviously, more homogeneous, the absolute nature of the harm done to the victim has more influence than more abstract notions of risk on dispositional policy for those convicted of these crimes.

Although offenders under twenty-one commit a disproportionate share of violent offenses, they do not dominate the statistics on such crimes as they dominate the statistics on offenses against property. Moreover, the violent crimes committed by the young are—on the average—less serious than those committed by young adults. Violent offenders under twenty-one are less often armed, and therefore pose a lower death risk in assaults and robberies they commit, than older offenders.[45] Adolescents who engage in both robbery and aggravated assault frequently do so in groups and thus generate more arrests per 100 crimes committed than do violent offenders over twenty.

Violent Crime in Juvenile Courts. One approach to juvenile court sentencing policy is to divide violent crime into three categories. The first category would include unarmed robbery and aggravated assault that either was provoked or did not produce grave bodily injury. For this group of offenses, maximum sentences in the juvenile justice system should be somewhat higher than maximum sentences for property offenses. Any presumption against formal processing should be limited to casual accessories or to trivial unarmed assaults and robberies, although probation or some other alternative to confinement could be available to first offenders.

The second category of violent offenses would include:

- robbery aggravated by the offender's use of a gun or a knife, or his infliction of injury serious enough to require hospitalization overnight

- assault aggravated by the use of a deadly weapon with intent to injure seriously
- attempted rape
- arson.

With these more serious offenses against the person, a maximum period of secure confinement twice that for property crime seems appropriate. Post-confinement supervision could be continued through an offender's twenty-first birthday or limited to a set period of time after adjudication. A *second* adjudication in the juvenile court for this class of offense could carry with it a presumption of some secure confinement with the explicit rationale of community protection.

The third category of violent crime would include:

- intentional criminal homicide (murder and manslaughter)
- attempted murder
- arson with intent to commit bodily harm
- rape.

Within the youth corrections system, maximum secure confinement would be limited to two and one-half years, and maximum supervision would continue until majority. Presumptive minimum sanctions also might be appropriate for such crimes. And juveniles over the age of fifteen previously adjudicated guilty of any offense in this class and again charged with an offense of this severity might face a strong presumption of waiver to the criminal courts.

Records of adjudication for the second and third categories of violent crime in the juvenile court should be only conditionally sealed. These records should be kept within the juvenile court but forwarded to police or prosecutors on request if the offender is charged with a felony within three years after his release from any custodial placement in the juvenile justice system. If three years pass without request, the records should be sealed or destroyed.

A policy of using relatively modest maximum sanctions, accompanied by a presumption of waiver for repetitively serious violent offenses, seems necessary in view of the informality and the limitations on the role of due process in juvenile court procedures. Within the age group under juvenile court jurisdiction, principal offenders in homicide and rape cases and repetitive offenders in the third category of violent crime are very rare. Those found guilty of such crimes should certainly incur more extensive sanctions, but for that very reason, the few juveniles charged with such crimes are entitled to all the procedural protections available to adults in the criminal justice system.

The disadvantages of a sentencing structure that retains jurisdiction in the juvenile court for serious offenses of violence concern the low maximum sanctions practically available in the juvenile court and the special pressures that serious, violent crimes place on community acceptance of the juvenile court as an institution appropriate for dealing with youth crime. For offenses such as murder and armed robbery, low maximum sentences lessen the capacity of the criminal justice system to incapacitate offenders from further crime in the community and may lessen the general deterrent effect of the legal threats directed at young offenders. And in some cases, the maximum punishment available in juvenile court may be less than the minimum punishment needed to satisfy the community's need for punishment appropriate to the offense.

It is this last point that creates stress on the entire juvenile court system. When the juvenile court sets penalties for cases of serious violence that are considered manifestly too lenient, the public may lose confidence in the juvenile court as an institution, not simply in the court's performance in this particular class of cases. The infrequent but well-publicized, outrageous offense—even though such offenses represent less than 2 percent of juvenile violent crimes—may be a substantial threat to the juvenile court's credibility, and could lead to public and legislative responses that are broad in scope and impact. These "deep-end" cases thus can pose a threat to the entirety of the juvenile court's mission.

Some Alternative Approaches.   The three most plausible alternative methods of dealing with violence in juvenile court are legislative determinations of presumptive minimum sanctions, fixed-price sentencing, and automatic waiver to the criminal court.

Minimum sentences seem more appropriate for some crimes of violence than for all other categories of crime in the juvenile court. The statutory definitions of aggravated assault and robbery are too vague to support presumptive or mandatory minimum sanctions, but two types of robbery and assault that might merit minimum presumptive sanctions are robbery in which the defendant was armed with a loaded gun or a knife or inflicted life-threatening injury and assault with a gun or knife, in which the defendant used life-threatening force. Crimes that fall within these subcategories might be considered to raise a presumption in favor of some custodial sentence, although the duration of a presumptive minimum custodial sentence and the range of facilities that might be used are open questions. But minimum sanctioning policies for these offenses may serve a valid purpose in a proportional system of juvenile sanctions. If the principle of proportionality justifies the juvenile justice system in limiting the punishment for trivial offenses, it also may justify imposing punishment for serious offenses.

Similarly, rape, arson with intent to commit bodily injury, willful killing, and attempted murder might appear to demand substantial secure confinement for any principal offender with the moral and intellectual equipment of the average mid-adolescent.

Under this scheme, the legislature or sentencing authority would set the presumptive minimum sanctions. Presumptive minimum legislation differs from "mandatory minimum" legislation in that the law acknowledges the power of court and prosecutor to deviate from the presumptive minimum. Since judges and prosecutors have the power to avoid mandated penalties in any event, "presumptive" legislation would more accurately reflect the realities of the sentencing situation.

Second, the law would not provide even presumptive minimum sanctions for accessories. Some juvenile accessories richly deserve the maximum sentence available in the juvenile court and even waiver to criminal court. But the label "accessory" probably encompasses too heterogeneous a group of defendants to support any firm concept of minimum accountability.

Presumptive sentencing legislation shifts punishment power from judges to the legislature. Removing power from those who make decisions in individual cases and giving power to elected officials who are removed from the system and operate on more abstract terrain where sentences are symbols may lead to escalation in penal sanctions.[46]

The polar opposite of the omnibus theory of delinquency is a system in which fixed punishments for each crime are chosen by the legislature or a sentence commission. The purpose of fixing sentences is to reduce the disparity between minimum and maximum sentences below the level achieved by legislated minimum sanctions. But fixed sentences are inappropriate for nonhomogeneous offenses, and they are especially inappropriate in a juvenile court system that bases specific punishment decisions on a mixture of motives. If incapacitation or deterrence were the predominant goals of juvenile justice sentencing policy, sentence ranges might be fairly readily fixed for serious offenses. But the very existence of a separate sentencing policy for juveniles implies that considerations of diminished individual capacity significantly affect the sentencing decision. The degree to which capacity is diminished by immaturity varies with the age and circumstances of each juvenile involved in a case. A fixed price approach represents either a rejection of notions of diminished capacity or the assignment of a fixed weight to individual immaturity as against judgments about the severity of the crime. The admission of diminished capacity as an explicit animating principle of sanctioning policy requires the provision of some leeway for individualization of justice.

In a number of states, a juvenile over a certain age (in Pennsylvania, age fourteen), arrested for murder or any of several other serious crimes, automatically falls under criminal court jurisdiction.[47] In some states, the criminal court may, at its discretion, refer the offender back to the juvenile court.[48]

Automatic waiver to the criminal court has the advantage of protecting that court from the political pressures that accompany such cases. It also assures to the defendant the protections accorded to all criminal defendants. But such a procedure is not a sentencing policy. The criminal court still needs a doctrinal basis for deciding what to do with such young offenders once they have been convicted.

Young Violent Offenders in Criminal Court.   Maximum sanctions for young violent offenders tried in criminal court should be higher than those for violent juvenile offenders but lower than those for violent adult offenders. Jurisdictions that retain or reintroduce capital punishment must evaluate the appropriateness of the death penalty for any criminal act committed by an individual under age twenty-one. A related question is whether extremely high prison sentences (in excess of ten years) should be confined to repetitively violent offenders who are principally responsible for the highest grade of murder in a particular jurisdiction.[49] A youth crime policy might include a provision that only those offenders under the age of twenty-one who are principally responsible for murder may receive prison sentences in excess of five years. Such a power would be based on the judgment that a sentence of more than five years of incarceration for an offender under age twenty-one implies that that individual is irredeemable. The decision on this question would affect sentencing policy for rape, armed robbery, accessorial liability for felony murder, and accessorial liability for criminal homicide.[50]

The principles of culpability, diminished responsibility, proportionality, and room to reform do not, themselves, dictate specific dispositional guidelines, age limits, or presumptions. The specific practices set forth above for youths convicted of property and violent crimes in juvenile and criminal court represent an effort to avoid, to the extent possible, the dangers of unwisely exercised discretion and of arbitrarily fixed rules. Accepting both the principles and the constraints, one might still argue for other practices.

Standards of Waiver

If the juvenile court is to survive as an institution, political pressures are likely to keep its jurisdictional age boundary relatively low—probably around sixteen—unless provision is made for waiver of accused individuals under the maximum jurisdictional age of the juvenile court when circumstances call for criminal court processing. New York and Vermont have survived for many years without any provision for waiving juveniles to adult criminal courts. Where the maximum age for juvenile court juris-diction is lower than seventeen, the legislative judgment of early adulthood reduces both the reasons for and the practical significance of waiver. Low jurisdictional age is, practically speaking, a "legislative waiver"—a whole-sale rather than a retail determination of adult criminal responsibility—which may overload the criminal courts. Waiver therefore seems prefer-able, although waiver policy is troublesome. No formal set of decisional principles now gives waiver a logical place in a coherent and coordinated social policy toward youth crime.

Coordinating youth crime policy would lower the stakes of the waiver decision. A policy of age-graded sentencing in both juvenile and criminal courts would diminish the impact of waiver to the criminal court. The dif-ference that waiver would make for a given offender would not be between two years and life imprisonment[51] but rather between two-and-a-half years and five years. The waiver decision would still be fateful, nonetheless, and it should therefore be made on a principled basis.

Previous sections have discussed existing and proposed standards for waiver to the criminal court. In Chapter II, it was noted that long lists of guidelines are unhelpful and employ questionable criteria. Chapter IV argued that the extraordinarily narrow waiver provision advocated in the tentative draft of the Juvenile Justice Standards Act relied too heavily on the accused's past criminal record rather than on the present charge.

A substantive standard for waiver might, following a finding of probable cause, ask a single question:

Is the existing range of juvenile court sanctions clearly insufficient should this defendant be convicted?

In jurisdictions that use the eighteenth birthday as the border of juvenile court jurisdiction, this standard would probably confine waiver cases to murder, attempted murder, forcible rape, repetitive armed robbery, and multiple sales of hard narcotics. This, at least, is my estimate of how appellate courts would interpret such a standard. One of the advantages of this single standard is that it is likely to generate a common law of waiver based on proportionality of punishments for young offenders as cases are litigated in appellate courts. In different jurisdictions, the standard might be interpreted in different ways, but it would at least impose some rule of law on the waiver decision.

The applicability of waiver to juvenile accessories is a complex question. Anglo-American criminal law imposes equal liability on those who aid, abet, assist, or encourage the principal offender in the commission of a criminal act. This criminal liability extends not only to acts that have been agreed upon but to the "reasonably foreseeable" consequences of those acts and to liability for murder whenever a killing takes place during the course of a forcible felony, such as robbery, burglary, or arson.[52]

But typically, even serious crimes committed by adolescents are substantially unplanned events that involve small or medium-sized groups of offenders.[53] Such acts are very different from the classic criminal conspiracies for which the concept was designed; not infrequently, in such cases, adolescents find themselves on the difficult borderline between participating in a criminal act and simply being part of a group that was present when a crime was committed. Indiscriminate use of the doctrine of accomplice liability with adolescents may burden them with criminal liability for nothing more than the company they keep. The principle of equal culpability between the robber with the gun and his street-corner companions seems suspect, and the extraordinary susceptibility of all adolescents to peer pressure might be considered as another factor in mitigation of the full-accomplice liability of mid-adolescents.

Accessorial liability is one of many issues that would be hammered out during the evolution of a common law of waiver directed specifically at the issue of minimum social need for punishment. Other issues of importance include the offender's age and emotional maturity. But all of these factors must be measured against a single standard: minimum social necessity of punishment.

Procedural Aspects of Substantive Reforms

Changes in the substance of sentencing policy toward young offenders are likely to produce changes in court—particularly juvenile court—procedures involving young offenders. For example, some years ago, the restriction of liberty that could follow from being labeled "delinquent" was the basis for extension of the right to counsel and the requirement that delinquent acts must be proved beyond a reasonable doubt.[54] Similarly, open recognition that the juvenile court aims to punish young offenders may put additional pressure on courts to provide persons accused in the juvenile court with procedural guarantees that parallel those provided in the criminal court. Yet the movement toward increased formality of process will confront two countervailing forces: the huge volume of youth arrests and the value that both the system and young offenders derive from informal processes coupled with limited doses of social control. What is likely to emerge is a two-track system in which most cases are resolved without complete formal processing, while an important minority of cases involving very serious offenses are resolved by adversary processes closely resembling full dress criminal trials. The further extension of due process guarantees would not reverse the current trend toward informal procedures, but might well affect the implementation of substantive reforms.

Controlling Sentencing Disparity

Any system that makes the sentence of the court discretionary carries with it the risk of sentence disparity—equally culpable offenders receiving different sentences because they appear before different judges. Systems of presumptive sentences, proposed to reduce disparity, are inappropriate, for a variety of reasons, for the juvenile system.[55]

But less heroic reforms can help to reduce sentence disparity. The range of available sanctions for particular crimes can be narrowed. And other institutional changes can further reduce the disparities that remain in a system that gives the judge the opportunity to choose between community supervision and a custodial placement in a large number of cases. Two institutional changes that have been proposed for this purpose are providing rights to counsel at dispositional hearings and to appellate review of sentences. Dispositional hearings are often of more consequence to young offenders than the hearings at which they are adjudicated delinquent. But because lawyers are not of uniform quality, the effects of representation at the hearing on sentencing disparity are difficult to predict. Appellate review also is no panacea for sentencing disparity. Appellate judges are likely to give sentencing judges wide latitude in exercising discretionary power; moreover, appeals take time and would be relatively rare in juvenile court cases.[56]

Some less obvious institutional arrangements may have more dramatic effects on sentencing disparity. The first of these is the dissemination of information to bench and bar about how different types of cases are normally treated. Information of this sort gives the judge informal guidelines and provides prosecution and defense attorneys with valuable ammunition in the dispositional hearing and at the appellate level.

Another method of reducing disparity is to give a centralized correctional administration power to determine where a sentenced offender is sent and the length of his or her stay. If reducing disparity is its explicit goal, such centralized power can be very effective in eliminating patterns of disparity, for example, between urban and rural jurisdictions. But if correctional administrators see their mission as rehabilitation, increasing their power may increase disparity, rather than achieving a system of proportional punishments.[57] Here, as in so many other facets of criminal justice, the attitudes and capacities of particular participants in the system may dictate the appropriate path to reform. Policies that increase disparity in one system may reduce disparity in another. The particular circumstances of police, courts, and corrections are important variables to be considered in the allocation of power.

Sentencing Criteria and Correctional Motives

The sentencing criteria discussed above do not include the offender's need for rehabilitative services as a rationale for the exercise of social control. This rationale is, however, irrelevant to the aims, staffing, and structure of those facilities, secure and nonsecure, to which young offenders will be referred. If there is any meaning to a social policy that gives offenders room to reform, the facilities in which they spend their time should be decent, not overcrowded, and contain a variety of educational, vocational, medical, and counseling programs that have as an explicit goal helping the offender to help himself. To the extent possible, the institution would de-emphasize security needs and be community-based.

The extent to which participation in education, counseling, and medical treatment programs should be compulsory is debatable. But efforts to provide smaller, better, more humane institutions and meaningful opportunities to participate in self-improvement programs are essential to any rational sentencing scheme. Principles and guidelines for sentencing youthful offenders can only be as good as the facilities to which the offender is sentenced. In this important sense, reform in dispositional policy is intimately connected to the institutions that deliver that policy.

* * *

The need for reform in both juvenile and criminal courts remains painfully obvious. The decline in acceptance of the omnibus theory of delinquency renders the juvenile court particularly vulnerable to arguments for its total abolition. But any institution that deals with young offenders will face the problems associated with social policy toward youth crime. The successors to the juvenile court might therefore be very similar to its predecessor. Francis Allen was probably correct when he stated, some years ago: "The processes of the [juvenile] court, with all their limitations may still represent the best and least harmful method that our civilization has devised to handle these problems."[58]

Notes

Introduction

1. Glen Elder, Jr., "Adolescence in the Life Cycle: An Introduction," *Adolescence in the Life Cycle: Psychological Change and Social Context,* ed. by Sigmund Dragastin and Glen Elder, Jr. (Washington, D.C.: Hemisphere Publishing, 1965), p. 3.

Chapter I

1. President's Commission on Law Enforcement and Administration of Justice, *The Challenge of Crime in a Free Society* (Washington, D.C.: U.S. Government Printing Office, 1967), p. 35.

2. For a definition of Index Crimes, see Department of Justice, Federal Bureau of Investigation, *Uniform Crime Reports 1976* (Washington, D.C.: U.S. Government Printing Office, 1977), pp. 34–35.

3. For data on the concentration of multiple offender criminal activities among the young, see U.S. Department of Justice, Law Enforcement Assistance Administration, *Criminal Victimization in the United States, 1973: A National Crime Survey Report* (Washington, D.C.: U.S. Government Printing Office, 1967), p. 66, note 1.

4. James Q. Wilson, *Thinking About Crime* (New York: Basic Books, 1975), pp. 199–201.

5. Norval M. Morris, *The Future of Imprisonment* (Chicago: University of Chicago Press, 1974), pp. 31–37, 62–73.

6. U.S. Department of Justice, Law Enforcement Assistance Administration (LEAA), *Criminal Victimization in the United States, 1973,* pp. 35–37.

7. Marvin Wolfgang, Robert Figlio, and Thorsten Sellin, *Delinquency in a Birth Cohort* (Chicago: University of Chicago Press, 1972).

8. C. W. Parsons, *America's Uncounted People* (Washington, D.C.: U.S. Government Printing Office, 1972); David M. Heer, ed., *Social Statistics and the City* (Cambridge: MIT Press, 1967).

9. During the period 1965–75, clearance rates for burglary decreased from 24.7 percent to 17.5 percent and for robbery from 37.6 percent to 27.0 percent on a national basis. Clearance rates for larceny were stable. Compare Department of Justice, Federal Bureau of Investigation, *Uniform Crime Reports, 1965* (Washington, D.C.: U.S. Government Printing Office, 1966), Table 8; and Department of Justice, Federal Bureau of Investigation, *Uniform Crime Reports, 1975* (Washington, D.C.: U.S. Government Printing Office, 1976), Table 19.

10.   Franklin E. Zimring, "Dealing with Youth Crime: National Needs and Federal Priorities," Report to the Coordinating Council on Juvenile Justice and Delinquency Prevention (1975), p. 30. The statistics reported in Table I-5 already incorporate recent increases in female arrests. While changing patterns of young female criminality deserve sustained study, any social policy that results in the deemphasis of social-control resources on status offenders and runaways will probably decrease the number of females formally processed by the courts and involved in youth corrections.

11.   See Robert Vinter et al., *Time Out: A National Study of Juvenile Correctional Programs* (Ann Arbor: University of Michigan, Institute of Continuing Legal Education, 1976), p. 42.

12.   During the period 1965–75, the ratio of city to suburban Part-I-offense arrests decreased from 4.6:1 to 2.7:1. During that same period, the city-to-suburban ratio for the violent offenses of homicide, robbery, and rape decreased more modestly from 7.2:1 in 1965 to a level of 4:1 in 1975. Controlling for shifts in the youth population, the arrest rates for Index Crimes decreased from 1.5 city/suburban in 1965 to 1.3 in 1975. For the three violent offenses, the arrest rate difference moved from 2.4 to 2.0. Aggravated assault is excluded from this analysis because the definition of the behavior may vary from urban to suburban areas.

   A more detailed analysis of the *Uniform Crime Report, 1974,* computed by Arthur Stinchcombe, reveals the following crime-specific ratios:

Ratio	Offense						
	Homicide	Robbery	Rape	Aggravated Assault	Burglary	Larceny	Auto Theft
Over 250,000 / Rural Area	2.8	28.6	4.2	3.2	2.8	3.3	9.6
Over 250,000 / Suburban Area	3.8	7.3	2.9	2.3	1.8	1.3	2.9
Over 1 million / 250,000 to 500,000	1.4	1.9	1.1	1.3	0.8	0.7	1.3
Suburban Area / Rural Area	0.7	3.9	1.5	1.4	1.6	2.5	3.3

Chapter II

1.   *New York Family Court Act,* § 712(a) (1975).

2.   *New Jersey Stats. Annot.,* 2A:43 (1952); 11 *Penn. Stats.,* § 50-102 (1930).

3.   Mark Levin and Rosemary Sarri, *Juvenile Delinquency: A Comparative Analysis of Legal Codes in the United States* (Ann Arbor: National Assessment of Juvenile Corrections, 1974), pp. 19–23.

4.   See the discussion in ibid., Section 2, Part B, note 3. The substantive standards for waiver have recently and accurately been characterized as "no more than lists of the competing policies any juvenile court must weigh in deciding to waiver (*sic*) jurisdiction." See, e.g., *Tenn. Code Annot.,* § 37-234 (1977):

       Transfer from juvenile court.—(a) After a petition has been filed alleging delinquency based on conduct which is designated a crime or public offense under the laws, including local ordinances, of this state, the court, before hearing the petition on the merits, may transfer the child to the sheriff of the county to be held according to law and to be dealt with as an adult in the criminal court of competent jurisdiction. The disposition of the child shall be as if he were an adult if:

(1) The child was sixteen (16) years or more of age at the time of the alleged conduct, or the child was fifteen (15) or more years of age at the time of the alleged conduct if the offense charged included murder, manslaughter, rape, robbery with a deadly weapon, or kidnapping;

(2) A hearing on whether the transfer should be made is held in conformity with § § 37-224, 37-226;

(3) Reasonable notice in writing of the time, place and purpose of the hearing is given to the child and his parents, guardian, or other custodian at least three (3) days prior to the hearing; and,

(4) The court finds that there are reasonable grounds to believe that:
(i) The child committed the delinquent act as alleged;
(ii) The child is not commitable to an institution for the mentally retarded or mentally ill; and,
(iii) The interests of the community require that the child be put under legal restraint or discipline.

(b) In making the determination required by subsection (a) of this section, the court may consider, among other matters:

(1) The extent and nature of the child's prior delinquency records;

(2) The nature of past treatment efforts and the nature of the child's response thereto;

(3) Whether the offense was against person or property, with greater weight in favor of transfer given to offenses against the person;

(4) Whether the offense was committed in an aggressive and premeditated manner; and

(5) The possible rehabilitation of the child by use of procedures, services and facilities currently available to the court in this state.

5.   Alabama (*Code of Alabama,* 13A § 5-101 1975 Interim Supp.); Florida (*Florida Stats. Annot.,* § 39.01 1974); Kentucky (*Kentucky Rev. Stats.,* § 208.020 1977); Maine (*Maine Rev. Stats. Annot.,* 15 § 2502 1975 Supp.); Maryland (*Annot. Code of Maryland,* § 3-801 1974); Nebraska (*Stat. of Nebraska,* § 43-202 1945); New Hampshire (*New Hampshire Rev. Stats. Annot.,* § 169.2 1975 Supp.); Oklahoma (*Oklahoma Stats. Annot.,* 10 § 1101 1936); South Carolina (*Code of Laws of South Carolina,* § 14-21-20 1975); Wyoming (*Wyoming Stats.,* § 14.115.4ii 1957). Mark Levin and Rosemary Sarri, *Juvenile Delinquency,* pp. 13–14. Hunter Hurst of the National Center for State Courts provided data on current jurisdictional practice.

6.   Ibid. Alabama and Oklahoma raised jurisdictional age from sixteen to eighteen; Florida, Maine, Maryland, and New Hampshire raised maximum jurisdictional age from seventeen to eighteen. Kentucky and Nebraska lowered jurisdictional age from eighteen to sixteen, while South Carolina reduced maximum jurisdictional age from eighteen to seventeen. See also Levin and Sarri, op. cit.

7.   Delinquency jurisdiction until age eighteen is recommended by the *Uniform Juvenile Court Act* (National Conference of Commissioners on United States Laws, 1968); *Model Act for Family Courts* (U.S. Department of Health, Education and Welfare,

Washington, D.C., 1975); and the *Task Force to Develop Standards and Goals for Juvenile Justice and Delinquency Prevention, Standards* (Washington, D.C.: U.S. Government Printing Office, 1976). The IJA/ABA *Tentative Draft* would extend delinquency jurisdiction to children under age eighteen at time of offense or age twenty at initiation of court proceedings. IJA/ABA Juvenile Justice Standards Project, *Standards Relating to Juvenile Delinquency and Sanctions* (Cambridge, Mass.: Ballinger Publishing Co., 1977). There is typically little commentary and there are few statements of rationale for these standards.

8.   Rollins M. Perkins, *Perkins on Criminal Law* (Mineola, N.Y.: Foundation Press, 1969), p. 837.

9.   President's Commission on Law Enforcement and Administration of Justice, *Task Force Report: Juvenile Delinquency and Youth Crime* (Washington, D.C.: U.S. Government Printing Office, 1967), pp. 2–4.

10.   Ibid., p. 3.

11.   Julian Mack, "The Juvenile Court," *Harvard Law Review,* XXIII (1909), p. 107.

12.   Ibid., pp. 107–108; but see Mack, p. 109, on waiver to criminal court.

13.   *Illinois Juvenile Court Act, Illinois Rev. Stats.,* §§ 702-5 and 702-4 (1965).

14.   President's Commission on Law Enforcement and Administration of Justice, *The Challenge of Crime in a Free Society* (Washington, D.C.: U.S. Government Printing Office, 1967), p. 84.

15.   Ibid.

16.   Sanford Fox, *The Law of Juvenile Courts in a Nutshell* (Minneapolis: West Publishing Company, 1977), pp. 65–67; *New York Family Court Act,* §§ 110 et seq. (1975).

17.   *Illinois Juvenile Court Act, Illinois Rev. Stats.,* §§ 702-5 and 702-4 (1965); *New York Family Court Act,* §§ 110 et seq. (1975); *Basic Juvenile Court Act, Rev. Code of Washington Annotated* (Supplement, 1977), Ch. 291.

18.   According to the 1920 report of the charity service for Cook County, Illinois, probationary orders outnumbered institutional orders in delinquency cases by six to five in 1905, the first year for which data are reported. Probationary orders outnumber "cases . . . to institutions and associations" in seven of the eight years covered by the reports. *Charity Service Reports,* Cook County, Illinois (1920), p. 252. A qualitative report of policy appeared in the *Juvenile Court Record,* vol. 4, no. 8 (August 1903), in a report by the Honorable Richard A. Tuthill:

> In cases of delinquent children, the court always endeavors to avoid anything that would make the young offenders feel that they are before a judge. The first time the boy or girl is brought into court they are given a good forcible talk. The habits and home environment are inquired into and a probation officer is appointed to look after the case.

The motives and functions of the juvenile court movement have been the subject of lively debate among contemporary historians, e.g., Anthony Platt, *The Child Savers: The Invention of Delinquency* (Chicago: University of Chicago Press, 1969); Sanford Fox, "Juvenile Justice Reform: An Historical Perspective," *Stanford Law Review,* Vol. 22 (1970), pp. 1187–1239; Stephen Schlossman, *Love and the American Delinquent: The Theory and Practice of "Progressive" Juvenile Justice 1825–1920* (Chicago: University of Chicago Press, 1977).

19.   See *In Re Gault* 387 U.S. 1 (1967). But see also the data reported in Figure II-2, and

Lawrence E. Cohen, *Delinquency Dispositions: An Empirical Analysis of Processing Decisions in Three Juvenile Courts* (Washington, D.C.: U.S. Government Printing Office, 1975); Rosemary Sarri, *Brought to Justice? Juveniles, the Courts, and the Law* (Ann Arbor: National Assessment of Juvenile Corrections, 1976), pp. 69–70, which indicates that courts are likely to handle approximately 50 percent of their cases nonjudicially.

20.   See Figure II-2, and Lawrence E. Cohen, op. cit. The President's Task Force on Juvenile Delinquency and Youth Crime found that probation was used in 49 percent of adjudicated delinquency cases. President's Commission on Law Enforcement and Administration of Justice, *Task Force Report.*

21.   Charles E. Lister, "Privacy, Recordkeeping, and Juvenile Justice," *Pursuing Justice for the Child,* ed. by Margaret Rosenheim (Chicago: University of Chicago, 1976). An unpublished summary of state legal codes estimates that more than half of all states have statutes protecting court and police records from disclosure, although many of the statutes permit access in special circumstances. Joseph Austin et al., "A Summary of State Legal Codes Governing Juvenile Delinquency," Center for the Study of Criminal Justice Policy, 1977, Table II.

22.   President's Commission on Law Enforcement and Administration of Justice, *Task Force Report.*

23.   Paul Nijelski, "Diversion: Unleashing the Hound of Heaven?," *Pursuing Justice for the Child,* p. 95; Irving Pilliavin and Scott Briar, "Police Encounters with Juveniles," *American Journal of Sociology,* LXX (1964), p. 209.

24.   Rosemary Sarri, op. cit., pp. 69–70.

25.   President's Commission on Law Enforcement and Administration of Justice, *Task Force Report,* p. 5.

26.   Patricia Wald, "Pretrial Detention for Juveniles," *Pursuing Justice for the Child,* pp. 120–122.

27.   *Ill. Rev. Stats.,* Chap. 37, § 703-6(2) (1975); *New York Family Court Act,* § 739 (1975); but see *Arizona Rev. Stats.,* § 8-226A (1963), which provides for detention of alleged delinquent or incorrigible children "when necessary."

28.   Secure detention is generally defined as "the temporary care of children who require secure custody for their own or the community's protection in physically restricting facilities, pending court disposition." William H. Sheridan, *Standards for Juvenile and Family Courts* (U.S. Department of Health, Education and Welfare, 1966), p. 23.

       At the time of the 1974 LEAA census of juvenile facilities, 25,397 children were in training schools and 11,010 in detention. The average duration of detention was ten days; the average stay in training school was 239 days. On the basis of the census figures and averages, an estimated 38,848 children were committed to training schools and 393,543 were detained annually. Department of Justice, LEAA National Criminal Justice Information and Statistics Service, *Children in Custody: Advance Report on the Juvenile Detention and Correctional Facility Census of 1974* (Washington, D.C.: U.S. Government Printing Office, 1977).

29.   Paul Nijelski, op. cit., p. 95. The figures noted in the quotation are rough estimates by Nijelski.

30.   Rosemary Sarri, op. cit., pp. 69–71. As an example, the *1977 Plan of the Wisconsin Council on Criminal Justice* reports that, in the ten regions in that state, the percentage of cases referred to the juvenile court that were handled informally varied dramatically. Region I handled only a quarter of its juvenile court intakes on an informal basis, while four of the ten regions handled in excess of 60 percent of all cases referred to the court

informally. City size and case loads appear to be insufficient explanations for this kind of variation because Region VIII (including Madison, Wisconsin) handled 65 percent of its cases on an informal basis while Region IX (including Racine and Kenosha, Wisconsin) handled only 35 percent on an informal basis. Much remains to be learned about the determinants of juvenile court case dispositions. Wisconsin Council on Criminal Justice, *1977 Plan,* Appendix L (1977).

31.   Rosemary Sarri, op. cit., p. 70.

32.   Ibid., pp. 152, 212–214.

33.   Ibid., p. 214.

34.   Diversion programs within the juvenile court are a growth industry, but neither precise counts of juveniles enrolled in formal pretrial diversion nor a precise definition of what a formal diversion project is are available. It is also worth noting that diversion programs in the criminal courts tend to specialize in youthful offenders. Franklin E. Zimring, "Measuring the Impact of Pretrial Diversion from the Criminal Justice System," *University of Chicago Law Review,* Vol. 41 (Winter 1974), p. 224. National Center for Social Statistics, *Juvenile Court Statistics* (Washington, D.C.: U.S. Department of Health, Education and Welfare, 1975), p. 3. See also Joan Mullin et al., *Pre-Trial Intervention: A Project Evaluation of Nine Man-Power Based Pre-Trial Intervention Projects* (Cambridge, Mass.: Abt Associates, 1974).

35.   Even in jurisdictions that require a hearing before a formal detention order, juveniles may be detained before a final intake decision is made either in police custody or in a juvenile correctional facility under "emergency conditions." There is also a legal recognition of "interim detentions" before a formal hearing. Patricia Wald, op. cit., p. 120.

There is no way to determine how many of the hundreds of thousands of detentions that occur annually are motivated by the desire to punish or to "teach the young offender a lesson," but the practice is probably common in many juvenile justice systems.

Punitive detention is wrong and may be unconstitutional, but it is also very difficult to control. Granting young offenders bail rights equivalent to those of adults will not, by itself, reduce the use of detention. Studies of money bail in criminal courts suggest that more comprehensive reforms are necessary. See William Landes, "The Bail System: An Economic Approach," *The Journal of Legal Studies,* II (1973), p. 79. Caleb Foote, "The Coming Constitutional Crisis in Bail: Part I and II," *University of Pennsylvania Law Review,* CXIII (1969), p. 959 (Part I) and p. 1125 (Part II).

Short-term punitive detention is particularly difficult to control. Police and intake workers have discretion prior to the period where a judicial hearing is practical, and punitive motives are difficult to isolate. A money damage legal remedy for wrongful loss of liberty would probably not be terribly effective, if experience with tort remedies for unlawful searches is applicable to this area. See William Geller, "Enforcing the Fourth Amendment: The Exclusionary Rule and Its Alternatives," *Washington University Law Quarterly* (1975), p. 691.

Yet much can be done to reduce the use of punitive detention even at early stages, particularly if court administrators are sympathetic to this goal. First, judges can admonish police and intake workers in appropriate detention cases when and if they reach the court. Second, alternatives to secure detention can be created and well publicized. The availability of such alternatives would make the use of a secure facility easier to question and harder to justify. Third, legislation and court rules can put narrow limits on what is considered "short-term" and shorten the time limit for detention without a judicial hearing. The more quickly a detention hearing is required, the easier the task of controlling punitively motivated detention.

The detention hearing should be considered a "critical stage" of the delinquency proceeding. The juvenile should have a right to counsel, and the judge should be required to give reasons for continuing the detention. This procedural change would reduce detention both by providing an earlier check on discretion and by upping the cost—to the court and police—of using secure detention. In the long run, controlling punitive detention requires convincing some judges and lawyers to work weekends and evenings. That type of organizational change may be of more consequence than the presence or absence of a legal right to bail and is too often overlooked in the literature on law reform. I have found, for example, that of the defendants who appeared eligible for the Manhattan Court Employment Project (a program that involved finding jobs for and dismissing charges against selected, low-risk criminal defendants), those who were arrested on weekends were detained before trial at a rate 40 percent in excess of those arrested on weekdays. Franklin E. Zimring, "The Court Employment Project," A Report to the Bureau of Evaluation, Human Resources Administration, City of New York (1974), p. 18. My hypothesis was that the criminal justice system works longer hours than the criminal justice reform system.

The detention system also should be monitored on a continuing basis. A rate of "emergency" detention far in excess of detentions following formal hearing is a clear sign of trouble, just as a high ratio of preadjudication to postadjudication secure confinement suggests that the criteria for either the detention or the dispositional decision, are inappropriate. These judgments cannot be made unless the relevant data are collected, analyzed, and used on a continuing basis. For an example of the collection and dissemination of such data, see Leslie Wilkins et al., "Sentencing Guidelines: Structuring Judicial Discretion" (Albany: Criminal Justice Research Center, Inc., 1976).

36.   Rosemary Sarri, op. cit., pp. 69–71; National Center for Social Statistics, *Juvenile Court Statistics, 1973,* pp. 3–4, which suggests that an increase in serious offenses among juvenile offenders has led to an increase in juvenile handling. But see "Report of the Cook County Juvenile Court, 1973," in which a sample of one hundred first-time delinquency cases is traced through court processes, frequently to an indeterminate conclusion or informal supervision order.

37.   *Report of the Cook County Juvenile Court, 1973.*

38.   President's Commission on Law Enforcement and Administration of Justice, *Task Force Report,* p. 5; *Ill. Rev. Stats.,* Chapter 37, § § 704-1 to 704-8 (1975).

39.   *Ill. Rev. Stats.,* Chapter 37, § 705-2(b) (postadjudicatory) and § 703-6; *New York Family Court Act,* § § 754 (postadjudicatory and 720) (1975); *Basic Juvenile Court Act, Rev. Code of Washington Annotated* (Supplement, 1977), Chapter 291.

40.   *New York Family Court Act,* § 753 (1975); *Ill. Rev. Stats.,* Chapter 37, § 705-2(a) (1975).

41.   See Monrad Paulsen and Charles Whitebread, *Juvenile Law and Procedure* (Chicago: National Council of Juvenile Court Judges, 1974), pp. 151–166 for a summary of procedural requirements in adjudicatory proceedings.

42.   A survey of dispositional alternatives in New York City is indicative of this diversity. See Trude Lash and Heidi Sigal, *State of the Child: New York City* (New York: Foundation for Child Development, 1976), pp. 84–86.

43.   Robert Vinter, George Downs, and John Hall, *Juvenile Corrections in the States: Residential Programs and Deinstitutionalization* (Ann Arbor: National Assessment of Juvenile Corrections, 1975), pp. 16–18.

44.   Elizabeth Vorenberg and James Vorenberg, "Early Diversions from the Criminal Justice System: Practice in Search of Theory," *Prisoners in America,* ed. by Lloyd E.

Ohlin (Englewood Cliffs, N.J.: Prentice-Hall, 1973), p. 151. Franklin E. Zimring, "The Court Employment Project," Appendix II. Thirty-seven of the thirty-nine diversion projects operating in New York City handled offenders under age twenty-one. Sixteen of the pretrial diversion projects dealt only with offenders under age twenty-one.

45.   Doris Meisner of the United States Department of Justice advocated this approach, which has been incorporated in the new diversion project being administered by the Department of Justice.

46.   Norval M. Morris, *The Future of Imprisonment* (Chicago: University of Chicago Press, 1974), pp. 9–12.

47.   For example, the goals of the Manhattan Court Employment Project to divert criminal defendants were to:

> . . . convert . . . arrest from a losing to a winning experience—to build a bridge for the accused between the fractured world of the street and the orderly world of lawfulness and responsibility. The defendant wins because he gets a job he likes and the charges against him are dismissed . . . and society wins also because an individual who may be developing a criminal life-style has been converted into a working employee and taxpayer.

Vera Institute of Justice, Programs in Criminal Justice Reform, "Ten Year Report (1972), p. 80.

Writing in 1909, the judge called upon the state:

> . . . instead of asking merely whether a boy or girl has committed a specific offense, to find out what he is, physically, mentally, morally, and then if it learns that he is treading the path that leads to criminality, to take him in charge, not so much to punish as to reform, not to degrade but to uplift, not crush but to develop, not to make him a criminal but a worthy citizen.

Julian Mack, "The Juvenile Court," *Harvard Law Review,* XXIII (1909), p. 107.

48.   Some states, such as Alaska, have flat prohibitions on institutionalization of status offenders; other states, such as Ohio, require the judge to find the child unamenable to other forms of treatment before committing the child to a training school or other correctional facility. Still other states, such as New York, restrict the commingling of juvenile and adult offenders. Mark Levin and Rosemary Sarri, op. cit., pp. 10–12. *The Juvenile Justice and Delinquency Prevention Act of 1974* prohibits the assignment of status offenders to correctional facilities if states are to receive formula grants.

49.   The outgrowth of this discretion is considerable variation in rates of confinement. A 1974 study of rates of average daily institutional population for juveniles reports an extraordinary and not easily explicable variation among states in the rate per hundred thousand of total state population committed to juvenile institutions, camps, and ranches. The national average is 17.8 per 100,000 total state population. The five highest per capita rates are found in Wyoming, Nevada, Delaware, Tennessee, and New Mexico—not generally thought of as hotbeds of criminal activity. Such population centers as Illinois, Pennsylvania, Texas, Michigan, Massachusetts, and New York display the smallest rates of institutionalized delinquents within the definition of the study. The variation is substantial; Pennsylvania, with the highest jurisdictional ages within the sample, has a rate of institutionalization that is approximately a third of those of Nevada, Delaware, and Tennessee. Different crime rates are not the explanatory variable because there is no correlation between an individual state's rate of either total or property crime and the rate of juvenile incarceration. Robert Vinter, George Downs, and John Hall, op. cit., pp. 16–18.

50. Juveniles in New York and Vermont may not be transferred to adult court. (In both states, juvenile court jurisdiction ends at the sixteenth birthday.)

51. *Cook County Charity Service Report, 1920,* p. 253. The number of delinquents bound over to the grand jury increased to nearly twenty-five per year during 1915 and 1916. With the beginning of World War I, the numbers dropped precipitously to seven in 1917 and only two in 1918.

52. Lawrence Cohen, *Juvenile Disposition: Social and Legal Factors Related to the Processing of Denver Delinquency Cases* (Washington, D.C.: U.S. Government Printing Office, 1975).

53. Joel Eigen has found that fewer than 2 percent of the juveniles arrested for robbery are waived to adult courts. Joel Eigen, untitled Ph.D. dissertation in preparation, University of Pennsylvania, 1977; Franklin Zimring, Joel Eigen, and Sheila O'Malley, "Punishing Homicide in Philadelphia: Perspectives on the Death Penalty," *University of Chicago Law Review,* XLIII (Winter 1976), p. 227.

54. *Kent v. United States,* 383 U.S. 541 (1966).

55. Ibid., pp. 565–568.

56. *In Re Winship,* 397 U.S. 358 (1970) extended the standard of "proof beyond a reasonable doubt" to juvenile court proceedings.

57. Andrew von Hirsch, "Prediction of Criminal Conduct and Preventive Confinement of Convicted Persons," *Buffalo Law Review,* XXI (1971–1972), p. 717.

58. Franklin Zimring et al., "Punishing Homicide in Philadelphia," pp. 246–247.

59. President's Commission on Law Enforcement and Administration of Justice, *The Challenge of Crime in a Free Society,* p. 7.

60. William Landes, "The Bail System: An Economic Approach," *Journal of Legal Studies,* II (1973), p. 79.

61. The proportion of cases tried before a jury increases with the severity of the offense. In California, only 3 percent of misdemeanor cases are tried before juries. It is estimated that one out of seven felony cases is heard by a jury. Harry Kalven, Jr., and Hans Zeisel, *The American Jury* (Boston: Little, Brown and Co., 1966), pp. 17–19.

62. Ibid., pp. 19–22. For a discussion of the influence of the right to jury trial in homicide cases, see Franklin Zimring et al., op. cit., p. 237.

63. The severity of sentences is mitigated by parole practices, however. For example, the average sentence for robbery in Wisconsin was 71.4 months; the average time served in prison for that offense was 25.9 months. For burglary, the average sentence was 46.6 months; the average time served was 19.7 months. State of Wisconsin, Division of Corrections, *Daily Population Reports, 1971–1975.*

64. Adults convicted of robbery or burglary in Illinois can be sentenced to a maximum of twenty years imprisonment. Incarceration of juveniles for the same offense cannot be for more than eight years. Moreover, adults face a mandatory one-year minimum; there is no minimum sentence for juveniles.

65. Brian Forst of the Institute for the Study of Law and Social Research, Washington, D.C., provided these data.

66. *Youth Corrections Act,* 18 U.S.C. § 5017.

67. Persons sentenced under the Youth Corrections Act served 27.6 months for burglary; all other prisoners served 27.3 months for burglary. U.S. Department of Justice, Law Enforcement Assistance Administration, *Sourcebook of Criminal Justice Statistics, 1976* (Washington, D.C.: U.S. Government Printing Office, 1977), Table 6.83.

68. Ibid. In terms of average time served, young offenders serve approximately equal

sentences for robbery (27.5 months) and burglary (27.6 months), while adults served 27.3 months for burglary and 46.2 months for robbery.

69.   The data base for these comparisons is rather thin and subject to qualification. The number of Youth Corrections Act burglary sentences reported was seven, while 127 robbery sentences under the Youth Corrections Act were recorded during the same period. Since youthful offender terms are optional at the discretion of the judge, the more substantial robbery sentences may reflect greater perceived seriousness of offense.

70.   Paul Strassberg, *Violent Delinquents: A Report to the Ford Foundation* (New York: Ford Foundation, 1976), p. 154.

Chapter III

1.   Francis Allen, *The Borderland of Criminal Justice* (Chicago: The University of Chicago Press, 1964), p. 2.

2.   Julian Mack, "The Juvenile Court," *Harvard Law Review,* Vol. XXII (1909), p. 107.

3.   Juvenile Court of Cook County, *Annual Report* (1907), p. 123.

4.   Francis Allen, op. cit., pp. 51–52.

5.   Ibid., p. 53; President's Commission on Law Enforcement and Administration of Justice, *Task Force Report: Juvenile Delinquency and Youth Crime* (Washington, D.C.: U.S. Government Printing Office, 1967), pp. 12–16.

6.   President's Commission on Law Enforcement and Administration of Justice, *Task Force Report,* pp. 120–122.

7.   Ibid., pp. 226–228.

8.   *Wisconsin v. Yoder,* 406 U.S. 205 (1972); *Prince v. Massachusetts,* 321 U.S. 158 (1944).

9.   *Youthful Offender Act, Wis. Stats.* § 54.01: "Recognizing that [youthful offenders] are in their formative years with an adult lifetime ahead of them, it is to the advantage of society to concentrate on specialized treatment efforts."

10.   Geoffrey Hazard, "The Jurisprudence of Juvenile Deviance," in *Pursuing Justice for the Child,* ed. by Margaret Rosenheim (Chicago: University of Chicago Press, 1976).

11.   For example, 83 percent of youth charged with incorrigibility in Hennepin County, Minnesota (includes Minneapolis), were detained, compared with 77 percent charged with armed robbery, 60 percent charged with assault, and 51 percent charged with burglary. "Obviously, youth who have no home or whose parents refuse to accept them run the highest risk of detention regardless of what they have or have not done." Rosemary Sarri, *Brought to Justice? Juveniles, the Courts, and the Law* (Ann Arbor: National Assessment of Juvenile Corrections, 1976), p. 161. Those juveniles who are detained are significantly more apt to be accorded more severe dispositions than those who were released without being detained. Lawrence Cohen, *Juvenile Dispositions: Social and Legal Factors Related to the Processing of Denver Delinquency Cases* (Washington, D.C.: U.S. Government Printing Office, 1975), pp. 26–29.

12.   Close to 90 percent of all young persons have, at some time in their lives, engaged in some behavior that could form the basis for juvenile court jurisdiction. Frank Orlando and J. Block, "Classification in Juvenile Court: The Delinquent Child and the Child in Need of Supervision," *Juvenile Justice,* Vol. 23 (1974), p. 13. The President's Task Force on Juvenile Delinquency and Youth Crime estimated one in every nine children was referred to juvenile court for an act of juvenile delinquency before reaching age

eighteen. Among boys alone, the ratio is one to six. President's Commission on Law Enforcement and Administration of Justice, *Task Force Report,* p. 1.

13.   Jerome Miller and Lloyd Ohlin, "The New Corrections: The Case of Massachusetts," in *Pursuing Justice for the Child,* ed. by Margaret Rosenheim, pp. 155–157.

14.   Robert Vinter, ed., *Time Out: A National Study of Juvenile Correctional Programs* (Ann Arbor: National Assessment of Juvenile Corrections, 1976), pp. 62–63.

15.   Not all status offenses are outside the jurisdiction of the criminal courts: in states, such as New York, where the maximum juvenile jurisdiction is lower than the drinking age, liquor law violations by juveniles are heard in criminal court. Persons under twenty-one who purchase handguns also can be tried for violation of the Federal Gun Control Act. *Gun Control Act of 1968,* U. S. C. § 922(d)(3) (1970). See discussion, *infra,* in Subsection A of Section 5.

16.   *Alabama Code,* Title 15, § 266(1) et seq. (1958); *Connecticut Gen. Stat.* § 54-76(b) et seq. (1975); *Georgia Code* § 77-345 *et seq.* (1943); *New York Criminal Procedure Law,* § 720 et. seq. (1975); *Federal Youth Corrections Act,* 18 U.S.C. § § 5005-5024 (1970); *Wis. Stat.,* § 54.01 et seq. (1975).

As noted in the discussion in Chapter II, the sentences imposed under Youthful Offender Acts are actually longer in some cases.

Chapter IV

1.   Edwin M. Schur, *Radical Nonintervention: Rethinking the Delinquency Problem* (Englewood Cliffs, N.J.: Prentice-Hall, 1973).

2.   Jerome Miller and Lloyd Ohlin, "The New Corrections: The Case of Massachusetts," in *Pursuing Justice for the Child,* ed. by Margaret Rosenheim (Chicago: University of Chicago Press, 1976). Rosenheim had proposed "The New Corrections: Locking Them Out" as an alternate title for the article.

3.   Task Force to Develop Standards and Goals for Juvenile Justice and Delinquency Prevention, *Standard* 14115, 1976.

4.   Edwin M. Schur, op. cit., p. 169.

5.   Jerome Miller and Lloyd Ohlin, op. cit., p. 154.

6.   Ibid., pp. 163–164.

7.   *IJA/ABA Juvenile Justice Standards Project* (24 vols.; Cambridge, Mass.: Ballinger Publishing Co., 1977); Task Force to Develop Standards and Goals on Juvenile Justice and Delinquency Prevention, *Standards* (Washington, D. C.: U.S. Government Printing Office, 1976); National Advisory Commission on Criminal Justice Standards and Goals, *Courts* (Washington, D.C.: U.S. Government Printing Office, 1973).

8.   President's Commission on Law Enforcement and Administration of Justice, *Task Force Report: Juvenile Delinquency and Youth Crime* (Washington, D.C.: U.S. Government Printing Office, 1967), pp. 22–23.

9.   IJA/ABA Juvenile Justice Standards Project, *Standards Relating to Juvenile Delinquency and Sanctions* (Cambridge, Mass.: Ballinger Publishing Co., 1977), Standard 5.2; Task Force to Develop Standards and Goals for Juvenile Justice and Delinquency Prevention, *Standards,* Standards 14.13 and 14.14 (July 1976).

10.   The National Advisory Committee on Juvenile Justice and Delinquency Prevention favors immediate elimination of jurisdiction over noncriminal misbehavior. The

Advisory Committee on Standards would retain jurisdiction over noncriminal misbehavior while providing that juveniles not guilty of criminal misbehavior should not be held in secure custody. U.S. Department of Justice, LEAA, National Institute for Juvenile Justice and Delinquency Prevention, *Report of the Advisory Committee to the Administrator on Standards for the Administration of Juvenile Justice* (Washington, D.C.: U.S. Government Printing Office, 1976), pp. 11–16.

11.   Twenty-four months is the maximum sentence under the Juvenile Justice Standards. Juveniles waived to criminal court may face the death penalty under the standards set forth by the Advisory Committee on Standards. IJA/ABA Juvenile Justice Standards Project, *Standards Relating to Juvenile Delinquency and Sanctions* (Cambridge, Mass.: Ballinger Publishing Co., 1977), Standards 5.1-5.2; *Report of the Advisory Committee,* Standard 3.116.

12.   Edwin M. Schur, op. cit., pp. 145–146.

13.   IJA/ABA Juvenile Justice Standards Project, op. cit., Standard 4.2.

14.   U.S. Department of Justice, LEAA, National Institute for Juvenile Justice and Delinquency Prevention, op. cit., Standards 3.112 and 3.183.

15.   Juvenile Justice and Delinquency Prevention Act, 42 U.S.C. § 5601 et seq. (1970).

16.   IJA/ABA Juvenile Justice Standards Project, op. cit., Standards 5.1-5.2; Task Force to Develop Standards and Goals for Juvenile Justice and Delinquency Prevention, op. cit., Standards 14.13–14.14 (July 1976).

17.   Ministry of the Solicitor General, *Young Persons in Conflict with the Law: A Report of the Solicitor General's Committee on Proposals for New Legislation to Replace the Juvenile Delinquents Act* (Ottawa, Canada: Communications Division, Ministry of the Solicitor General, 1975).

18.   The average age of a runaway child in the United States is 14.5 years. Two-thirds of the runaway children arrested in the United States in 1975 were under age sixteen. Behavioral Research and Evaluation Corporation, *Final Report: The Incidence and Nature of Runaway Behavior* (Washington, D.C.: U.S. Department of Health, Education and Welfare, 1975).

19.   IJA/ABA Juvenile Justice Standards Project, *Standards Relating to Juvenile Delinquency and Sanctions,* Standard 1.1.

20.   Ibid. The volume contains no discussion of differential treatment for even the youngest children. The standards relating to juvenile delinquency and sanctions provide for a minimum-age jurisdiction of ten.

21.   See Chapter I, Table I-1.

22.   Franklin Zimring, Joel Eigen, and Sheila O'Malley, "Punishing Homicide in Philadelphia: Perspectives on the Death Penalty," *University of Chicago Law Review,* Vol. 43 (Winter 1976), pp. 246-247.

23.   Of the 152,000 violent crimes committed by young offenders (under twenty-one) in 1975, 133,000 were crimes of robbery or aggravated assault. Department of Justice, Federal Bureau of Investigation, *Uniform Crime Reports for the United States, 1975* (Washington, D.C.: U.S. Government Printing Office, 1976), Table 37.

24.   Sixty-four percent of the twelve- to nineteen-year-old victims of aggravated assault by a lone offender perceived their assailants to be between twelve and nineteen years old. Seventy percent of the twelve- to nineteen-year-old victims of aggravated assault by multiple offenders perceived their assailants to be between twelve and nineteen years old. U.S. Department of Justice, LEAA, National Criminal Justice Information and Statistics Service, *Criminal Victimization in the United States, 1973* (Washington, D.C.: U.S. Government Printing Office, 1976), pp. 85–87.

25. U.S. Department of Justice, LEAA. National Criminal Justice Information and Statistics Service, *Crimes and Victims: A Report of the Dayton-San Jose Pilot Survey of Victimization* (Washington, D.C.: U.S. Government Printing Office, 1974), pp. 130–131.

26. IJA/ABA Juvenile Justice Standards Project, *Standards Relating to Transfer Between Courts* (Cambridge, Mass.: Ballinger Publishing Co., 1977), Standard 2.2.

27. Ibid., Standard 2.2 (c) (2).

28. IJA/ABA Juvenile Justice Standards Project, op. cit., Standards 5.1-5.2.

29. For example, *Youthful Offender Act, Wis. Stats.,* §54.01 et seq. (1975).

30. IJA/ABA Juvenile Justice Standards Project, *Standards Relating to Juvenile Delinquency and Sanctions.*

31. The most careful study of the later careers of young offenders is being supervised by Marvin Wolfgang of the University of Pennsylvania. Preliminary results show that about half of all individuals arrested prior to age eighteen are arrested in the decade after their eighteenth birthday, but a far smaller proportion become chronic offenders.

32. James Coleman et al., *Youth: Transition to Adulthood* (Chicago: University of Chicago Press, 1974).

33. American Law Institute, *Model Penal Code,* §§ 4.01 (mental disease or defect) and 2.08 (intoxication) (1962).

34. *People v. Wolff,* 61 Cal. 2d 795, 394 P. 2d 959 (1964); *People v. Conley,* 64 Cal. 2d 310, 411 P. 2d 911 (1966); H. L. A. Hart, *Punishment and Responsibility* (Oxford: Clarendon Press, 1968), pp. 188–189.

Chapter V

1. See the discussion of PINS and delinquency in Chapter II, pp. 48–49.

2. Aidan Gough, Tentative Draft III, Juvenile Justice Standards Relating to Status Offenses (IJA/ABA Juvenile Justice Standards Project, 1975), p. 1. Other estimates are lower. The President's Task Force on Juvenile Delinquency and Youth Crime stated that "... status offenders account for over twenty-five percent of the total number of delinquent children appearing before children's courts and between twenty-five and thirty percent of the population of state institutions for delinquent children." President's Commission on Law Enforcement and Administration of Justice, *Task Force Report: Juvenile Delinquency and Youth Crime* (Washington, D.C.: U.S. Government Printing Office, 1967), p. 4.

3. For example, *Gun Control Act of 1968,* 18 U.S.C. § 925 (d) (2) (1970).

4. With respect to compulsory education, school attendance is a duty that both child and parent owe to the state, and a violation of that duty can be considered a breach of the law whether or not truancy is subsumed under the general rubric of delinquency. *People ι. Donner,* 302 N.Y. 857, 100 N.E. 2d 48 (1951); see *Wisconsin v. Yoder,* 406 U.S. 205 (1972).

5. *E.g., Michigan Comp. Law Annot.,* § 712 A.2 (1967).

6. *E.g., New York Family Court Act,* § 712 (b) (1975).

7. IJA/ABA Juvenile Justice Standards Project, *Standards Relating to Noncriminal Misbehavior* (Cambridge, Mass.: Ballinger Publishing Company, 1977); National Advisory Commission on Criminal Justice Standards and Goals, *Task Force Report:*

Courts (Washington, D.C.: U.S. Government Printing Office, 1973); Board of Directors, National Council on Crime and Delinquency, "Jurisdiction over Status Offenses Should Be Removed from the Juvenile Court: A Policy Statement," *Crime and Delinquency*, XXI (1975), p. 97; Richard Kobely and Betty Bosarge, International Association of Chiefs of Police, *Juvenile Justice Administration* (1973), p. 215.

8. "In view of the serious stigma and the uncertain gain accompanying official action, serious consideration should be given complete elimination from the court's jurisdiction of conduct illegal only for a child." President's Commission on Law Enforcement and Administration of Justice, *Task Force Report*, p. 27.

9. IJA/ABA Juvenile Justice Standards Project, *Standards Relating to Noncriminal Misbehavior*, Standard 3.2.

10. The constitutional dimensions of this issue have proved a major source of difficulty for the United States Supreme Court in recent years. *Bellotti v. Baird*, 429 U.S. 892 (1976); *Danforth v. Planned Parenthood of Central Missouri*, 428 U.S. 52 (1976); *Kremens v. Bartley*, 402 F. Supp. 1039 (vacated and remanded), __U.S.__ 97 S. Ct. 1709 (1977).

11. *Bellotti v. Baird*, 429 U.S. 892 (1976); *Prince v. Massachusetts*, 321 U.S. 158 (1944).

12. Trude Lash and Heidi Sigal, *State of the Child: New York City* (New York: Foundation for Child Development, 1976), pp. 83–86.

13. Ibid., pp. 125–127. Robert N. Mnookin, "Foster Care—In Whose Best Interests?" *Harvard Education Review*, XLIII.(1973), p. 599.

14. *E.g., Ill. Rev. Stats.*, Ch. 37, §§ 702-4 and 702-5 (1975). It is problematic whether a child who rejects his family is dependent in terms of juvenile court jurisdiction.

15. Such status offenders are not necessarily low on the list of priorities if the state's purpose is supervision. See Chapter II and Chapter V, pp. 84–85.

16. Young offenders are disproportionately involved in drug-law violations. Some reform literature encourages decriminalization of "victimless" crimes for the young. John Junker, Juvenile Justice Standards Project, Tentative Standards Draft, *Juvenile Crime* (IJA/ABA: 1974). This paper does not address the issue of either possession or sale of drugs by the young because policy prescriptions for young drug-law violators are intimately related to trends in the general treatment of the drug-law violators. To the extent that the possession or sale of drugs remains unlawful, the same conceptual basis for separate treatment of young offenders applies for drug laws.

17. IJA/ABA Juvenile Justice Standards Project, *Standards Relating to Juvenile Delinquency and Sanctions* (Cambridge, Mass.: Ballinger Publishing Company, 1977); IJA/ABA Juvenile Justice Standards Project, *Standards Relating to Non-criminal Misbehavior.*.

18. There were nearly 200,000 liquor-law violators under age twenty-one in 1975; 106,000 of these were under age eighteen. Of the 270,000-plus drug-law offenders under age twenty-one in 1975, almost 123,000 were under age eighteen. Department of Justice, Federal Bureau of Investigation, *Uniform Crime Reports for the United States, 1975* (Washington, D.C.: U.S. Government Printing Office, 1976), Table 37.

19. For example, 98,000 burglaries were reported in Chicago in 1974 and 1975, resulting in a total of eight victim fatalities. During the same period, half that number of robberies (48,343) produced a total of 385 victim deaths. Chicago Police Department, *Annual Reports, 1974–1975.*

20. Data provided by June Dorn of the Illinois Law Enforcement Commission.

21.   See Chapter II, pp. 50–52.

22.   John Harding, "Community Service Restitution by Offenders," in *Restitution in Criminal Justice,* ed. by Joe Hudson (Minneapolis: Minnesota Department of Corrections, 1977), p. 102.

23.   Joe Hudson, ed., *Restitution in Criminal Justice.* Work opportunities would seem a necessary part of a restitution program for unemployed youth.

24.   This issue is related to the general issue of punitive detention. See Chapter II, pp. 50–52.

25.   Caleb Foote, "The Coming Constitutional Crisis in Bail: Parts I and II," *University of Pennsylvania Law Review,* CXIII (1965), p. 959 (Part I), pp. 1125 (Part II).

26.   E.g., *Ill. Rev. Stats.,* Ch. 37, §705-10 (1975).

27.   IJA/ABA Juvenile Justice Standards Project, *Standards Relating to Juvenile Delinquency and Sanctions* (Cambridge, Mass.: Ballinger Publishing Company, 1977), Standards 5.1-5.2.

28.   Twentieth Century Fund, Task Force on Criminal Sentencing, *Fair and Certain Punishment—Report of the Twentieth Century Fund Task Force on Criminal Sentencing* (New York: McGraw-Hill, 1976).

29.   Presumably, prior record could not be used in making a punitive decision unless a youth's prior involvement with the juvenile court had culminated in an adjudication of guilt.

30.   Marvin E. Wolfgang, "Seriousness of Crime and a Policy of Juvenile Justice," in *Delinquency, Crime, and Society,* ed. by James F. Short (Chicago: University of Chicago, 1976), pp. 279–283.

31.   I presume that a point system would not count offenses that resulted in informal adjustment but would include the total number of points accumulated by convictions for multiple offenses resulting in a system logically similar to consecutive sentencing.

32.   *New York Family Court Act,* §753-2 (1975).

33.   In Cook County, Illinois, 1.7 percent of those juveniles arrested for auto theft are committed to state training schools. Information obtained from June Dorn, Illinois Law Enforcement Commission.

34.   Seven states and the federal government have Youthful Offender Acts.

35.   *New York Penal Law,* §70.00. *New York Criminal Procedure Law,* §720.10 (1975).

36.   Sentences under the youthful offender acts are typically indeterminate. An example of the policy is the New York Criminal Procedure Law, §720.10 (1975).

37.   Chapter III, pp. 68–69. *Federal Youth Corrections Act,* 18 U.S.C. §§ 5005–5024 (1970). *Wis. Stats.,* §§ 54.01 et seq. (1975).

38.   Robert Martinson, "What Works? Questions and Answers about Prison Reform," *The Public Interest,* XXXV (1974), pp. 22–54.

39.   Norval M. Morris, *The Future of Imprisonment* (Chicago: University of Chicago Press, 1974), pp. 62–73.

40.   *Federal Parole Guidelines,* 28 C.F.R. Ch. 1, Part 2, §2.20 (1975).

41.   Franklin E. Zimring, "Making Punishment Fit the Crime: A Consumer's Guide to Sentencing Reform," *Occasional Papers,* University of Chicago Law School, No. 12 (1977).

42.   Franklin E. Zimring, "Determinants of the Death Rates from Robbery: A Detroit Time-Study," *Journal of Legal Studies,* Vol. VI, 2 (June 1977), pp. 317–322.

43.   Ibid.

44. Ibid.

45. Department of Justice, LEAA, National Criminal Justice Information and Statistics Service, *Crimes and Victims: A Report on the Dayton-San Jose Pilot Survey of Victimization* (Washington, D.C.: U.S. Government Printing office, 1974), p. 130.

46. Franklin E. Zimring, "Making Punishment Fit the Crime," pp. 13–17.

47. *Penn. Stat. Annot.,* Ch. 11, §50-303 (1973). Comment, "Youthful Offenders and Adult Courts," *University of Pennsylvania Law Review,* CXXI (1973), p. 1184.

48. For example, Pennsylvania allows for the transfer of murder cases back to the juvenile court from the criminal court. If the child is convicted in the criminal court of a crime less than murder, the case may be transferred to the juvenile court for disposition. *Penn. Stats. Annot.,* Ch. 11, §50-303 (1973).

49. For an analysis of current sentencing practices for homicide, see Franklin Zimring, Joel Eigen, and Sheila O'Malley, "Punishing Homicide in Philadelphia: Perspectives on the Death Penalty," *University of Chicago Law Review,* Vol. 43 (Winter 1976).

50. Ibid., pp. 229–238, 245–247.

51. IJA/ABA Juvenile Justice Standards Project, *Standards Relating to Juvenile Delinquency and Sanctions,* Standards 5.1-5.2.

52. See, for example, *Ill. Rev. Stats.,* Ch. 38, §9-1(a)(3)(1975).

53. President's Commission on Law Enforcement and Administration of Justice, *Task Force Report,* p. 158.

54. American Bar Association, Project on Minimum Standards for Criminal Justice, *Standards Relating to Trial by Jury* (New York: Office of Criminal Justice Project, Institute of Judicial Administration, 1968), pp. 1–2. Harry Kalven, Jr., and Hans Zeisel, *The American Jury* (Boston: Little, Brown and Co., 1966), p. 18. Vera Institute of Justice, *Felony Arrests: Their Prosecution and Disposition in New York City Courts* (New York: Vera Institute of Justice, 1977), p. 6.

55. Franklin E. Zimring, "Making the Punishment Fit the Crime," pp. 13–15.

56. In a recently completed study of sentencing review, Hans Zeisel and Shari Diamond estimate that 13 percent of all criminal defendants have appeals heard in Massachusetts and 17 percent of criminal defendants in Connecticut take their cases to higher courts. Sentence reduction after appellate review occurs in 2.3 percent of all criminal cases. Longer sentences are much more frequently appealed. The short sentencing frame in the juvenile court suggests that much lower rates of sentence appeal would emerge if sentencing review was applied to juvenile court dispositions. Hans Zeisel and Shari Diamond, "Sentencing Review in Massachusetts and Connecticut" (1977), p. 21.

57. David Fogel, *We are the Living Proof: The Justice Model of Corrections* (Cincinnati: W. H. Anderson, 1975). The Twentieth Century Fund Task Force Report on Criminal Sentencing, *Fair and Certain Punishment,* pp. 13–14.

58. Francis Allen, *The Borderland of Criminal Justice* (Chicago: University of Chicago Press, 1964), pp. 52–53.

Over the last decade, the issue of law and order has taken on fresh urgency. Crime rates have risen, and young men and women have been responsible for far more than their share of crimes. This disturbing development has called the entire system of juvenile justice into question. Juvenile courts and correctional institutions have been accused of being both lax and arbitrary, permanently stigmatizing youngsters for such trivial offenses as truancy and curfew violations, while providing a revolving door for teen-aged robbers, rapists, and murderers.

The Twentieth Century Fund Task Force on Sentencing Policy Toward Young Offenders has evaluated these charges and set forth principles for the administration of justice as it is meted out to offenders in late adolescence and